There is nothing written here
that has not been known before,
and I have no special skills in composition.
Therefore, I have no delusions
that this will greatly benefit anyone –
I have written this only to inspect my own mind
and examine my own understanding,
that the roots of my realizations and beliefs
may be strengthened,
and my determination to live in this Way
may be increased.

But if others
who now find these words in their hands
happen to find the same comfort and strength,
then may that merit be paid forward as well
and dedicated
to the salvation of all beings.[1]

THE
ENERGY
OF
GOD

LLOYD MATTHEW THOMPSON

STARFIELD

Starfield Press
Oklahoma City, OK

THE ENERGY OF GOD
by Lloyd Matthew Thompson
Copyright © 2019 Starfield Press - All Rights Reserved

First printing 2019
Second printing 2020

Paperback ISBN: 978-0-578-50788-0

Starfield Press
www.StarfieldPress.com
Oklahoma City, OK

Akasha Shore
www.AkashaShore.com

Cover design by Lloyd Matthew Thompson
Gate gate paragate parasamgate

THE
ENERGY
OF
GOD

For you.

I can never escape from you!
I can never get away from your presence!

If I go up to the heavens, you are there;
if I go down to the grave, you are there.

If I ride the wings of the morning,
if I dwell by the farthest oceans,
even there I find your presence,
even there your energy supports me.

I could ask the darkness to hide me
and the light around me to become night,
but even in darkness I cannot hide from you.

To you, the night shines as bright as day.

Darkness and light are the same to you.[2]

GENESIS

THE IMAGE OF GOD

IN THE BEGINNING WAS the Thought. And the Thought wanted more. And the more wanted the Thought. Because the Thought and the more were not separate, they instantaneously began to expand and take form. Each form existed to hold the Thought and express the Thought. The Thought held and expressed each form. The form was the Thought, and the Thought was the form.

The forming of the form caused no separation between the Thought and the form, but rather deepened the connection between the Thought and the form. The more that form expanded, the greater the connection between them grew, for once there has been unity, all parts of that unity are eternally connected, even if that unity is fragmented into countless unfathomable pieces.

This is what happened as soon as the Thought thought to form more. The very act of thinking created the form. Those forms then thought more forms, and those forms thought more forms, each form expanding and increasing the connection among all thoughts and forms.

And still no separation was found. The Thought remained aware of each and every fragment, just as every fragment was aware of the Thought.

The pure delight the Thought found in expanding itself began to give rise to something more than thought, something far past thinking—something beyond thought itself. The awareness of this newness had an unexpected and unforeseen effect on the Thought. The newness caused a spark, which grew into a fire that quickly engulfed and consumed the Thought, until it became the Thought itself. The Thought and the newness merged until there was no discernable difference between the two. It was then realized that the newness had always been the Thought, and the Thought had always been the newness. There had never been a newness at all, but instead the Thought had now seen and recognized a side of Itself that had been there all along.

The Thought named this newness *emotion*, and though it held a separate name, the Thought saw and understood that still no separation existed. Seeing how distinction held the ability to enhance experience and awareness while still causing no division, the Thought then further defined this particular emotion.

The emotion that delighted in expanding and experiencing, that was the first and defining awareness, and that was found to in fact identify the Thought at Its foundational core, was given the name *Love*.

Love was the reason for forming the form. Love was the Thought and the form. Love was the awareness *inside* each thought and each form—without which there *was* no thought and no form.

And the Thought saw that all was good, and exploded in joy, even deeper in love with all thoughts and all forms. The sheer force of this sparked all forms and all thoughts to increase their expansion and formation, and each thought also gave names to define all their own formations. The Thought found there was no limit to the expanse all things could reach, and no loss of connection, no matter the distance. The Thought found the farthest reaches were no different than Its own heart core. Near and far were one and the same. All things were one thing, no matter what name or idea or formation each took.

Each thought was immediately known by all other thoughts and forms, immediately experienced by all other thoughts and forms, immediately embraced by all other thoughts and forms. The constant and instantaneous perceptions of all awareness and all thought and all experience became a song to the Thought, and as all formations sang in united verse, the Thought named the all *Universe*.

The Universe played its music without pause, and with each note and each thought, each form shaped itself and named itself into whatever its own heart core desired. The heart of each fragment was an exact mirror image of the Thought's own heart. Each was a fraction, yet remained a whole—fully aware, fully alive, fully in love.

As the formations continued multiplying beyond imagination, no separation or division from the Thought was ever experienced, even when two forms seemed to oppose. Void and mass, light and dark, gas and liquid, hot and cold, up and down, motion and stillness all formed and existed effortlessly as a single myriad of thoughts, unseparated from one Thought. The Thought was with the all, the Thought was in the all, the Thought was the all.

Gradually, certain thoughts and forms began to focus more of their awareness on only the form they had formed and become. They began to forget they were a part of one greater Thought and form. The Thought was aware of every moment these fractions sang less and less, and watched as their distance grew. Rather than joining in the song of the whole, these fractals began to form veils and shrouds around themselves, keeping their song for themselves.

In focusing on only the forms and thoughts they had created, these images of the whole brought the experience of separation and division to the whole for the first time.

The Thought saw that even though these few chose to pretend they were separate from the whole, there was no true separation, yet still the Thought could not help experiencing the sensation of being separated from Itself through them. In a single moment, It knew both unlimited vastness and closed off loneliness.

With this, yet another sensation entered the awareness of the Thought. This sensation was not quite an emotion, but it was indeed a feeling. Layered in this feeling were many levels of other feelings — and none of them pleasing. These unpleasant feelings the Thought named *Pain* and *Suffering*. The pleasure of connection and the pain of separation became the first opposing sensations to truly oppose each other.

Though the separation was not really separation, the thoughts that chose to form such a double reality became so focused on their own reality they grew less and less aware of the Thought and the song of the Universe. This withdrawing of awareness also created the same imagined shroud between each individual thought form, disconnecting and isolating the individual from the individual, clearing the way for what became known as *violence, hatred,* and *dishonor* to exist for the first time.

Every other thought and form also experienced the separation and pain instantaneously. All were still one Universe, whether it was acknowledged or not. Some thoughts and forms adopted the illusion and wrapped themselves in shrouds as well. Other thoughts fled from such ideas and expanded further into oneness with the Universe.

Still, the Thought chose nothing but love, felt nothing but love for all these things and all these forms.

Yet even in the midst of enshroudment, some thoughts still remembered the Connection deep in their heart core, but they did not remember how to connect to the Connection. If ever they experienced moments of quietness and stillness, their hearts sobbed and cried out day and night for what it sensed was absent. These began trying everything they could imagine to reestablish the Connection they felt missing, and gain the attention of the Great Connection once again, though the attention had never truly wavered or been lost to them the entire time. The illusion was entirely one-sided.

In their efforts, these thoughts created every manner and method and action to try to reopen the Connection once again, holding *Faith* that it was possible to find again. Some of the methods invented seemed to work, while others turned out to create an even greater sense of separation.

As many enshrouded forms began to find ways to the Connection once again, a remembering began to spread to more and more enshrouded thoughts and forms, reconnecting those individual thoughts to each other, as well as to the Great Connection. In the presence of this rediscovered connection, the violence, hatred, and dishonor naturally fell away. As the Thought saw and felt all these things happening simultaneously, in continued love and joy It named this remembering *Hope*.

But many other thoughts, committed to an isolated separation, clinging to their familiar and safer-feeling forgetfulness, resisted all remembering, could not see or feel any connection, and fought to prove that their own forgetfulness was the only way. These thoughts truly felt — and feared — that any change from what was familiar to them would mean harm, death, the end of time.

Some thoughts even embraced both remembering and forgetting, deciding that the final remembering would not be until the end of days, and waited anxiously for that time with open arms.

Still others believed remembering could only come from outside, never from within their own heart core, and stood motionless, waiting for their rescue and reminding.

Yet there was never any moment that bright thoughts were not present, thoughts that arrived already fully connected to the Great Connection in the midst of even the darkest shrouds. The very presence of these thoughts and forms acted as reminder of Connection to all thoughts and forms simply by existing and living their full connection with the All. These forms naturally became messengers pointing the way toward the Great Connection, the Thought that is all thoughts, the Love that animates all thoughts and all forms. They lived their lives among the enshrouded, saying, *Do this, in remembrance*.

As each thought whose form was darkened by shrouds undertook the journey to reestablish their own connection for themselves, they too became natural beacons pointing the way to remembrance for all still guarding their song as if it were the entire Universe itself.

THE
ENERGY
OF
GOD

CONTENTS

Dear friends,
let us love one another,
for love comes straight from God.

Everyone who loves
truly knows God.

Whoever does not love
does not know God,
because

God is love.

No one has ever seen God,
but if we love,
God will be able to be seen in us,
and his love will be made complete
in us.

God is love.

Whoever lives in love
lives in God,
and God lives in them.

In this world,
we are God.[3]

PREFACE

GOD IS NOT A PERSON

I WAS RAISED IN church. I'm from the type of Protestant family who was at church every time the doors were open: every service, every event, every potluck buffet in the Fellowship Hall, and every early morning prayer meeting before work and school. My parents tell me that as a baby I learned to pull up and stand on my own to their singing the old hymn *Stand Up, Stand Up for Jesus,* and that *Jesus* was one of my first words spoken.

There was constant talk of God. Every aspect of life and every situation took God and *the right thing to do* into consideration. I was even pulled out of public schools to be homeschooled with curriculum that ensured it was a right and

Godly education. Church taught that if these right things to do were not followed, it was understood that when I died, I would be punished and thrown into *hell* — a place of being eternally tortured and burned in fire. If I successfully performed all the right things and worked hard to keep myself good enough, I was guaranteed to gain access into *heaven* and be happy for all eternity.

The type of God this painted for me was a God glaring down from above with a long list of *don't-do-this* rules, only loving and approving and accepting if certain conditions were met. This God I came to know is unfortunately the same God so many people still have demonstrated to them and are taught about — a disapproving, overly critical and judgmental God always watching for the slightest wrong to be done so that punishment can be dished out in the most harmful or humiliating way possible.

I was also taught there is a devil wandering the earth, trying everything he can do to get every person to *sin*, disobey, or do things *wrong*, so that they would be denied heaven and get hurled into hell where he would be the one to torture them for all eternity.

So on one side, I had a devil who was hell-bent on dragging me to hell, and on the other side, a God who seemed to be just itching to… also toss me into hell, for even my tiniest offense? Two super-entities floating over me, both battling to be the one to throw me into hell.

Even as a child, I always felt and knew something was not right about all these portrayals.

I've always been one to think for myself, feel into things for myself, and research for myself rather than simply taking someone's word. Beginning the solitary, self-motivated structure of being home-educated at seven years old only reinforced these attributes, and in this way, I'm very grateful for the sheltered life I had.

I did not understand how a God who was supposed to be a loving father, slow to anger, a gentle provider, and a mighty protector battling to save us from *going* to hell could at the same time be so unwaveringly harsh, quick to judge, and eager to strip away our resources in punishment. If God is supposed to *be* love and be unwilling for anyone to be destroyed in hell, then why does he act like such a jealous toddler and aggressive bully when someone doesn't do what he wants? Why do his supposed followers — his representatives in this place — severely discriminate against and violently attack and reject others who are not like them?

How can the same breath announce that God is both love and hate at the same time?

This doesn't sound very enlightened *or* loving.

I left the church around age twenty-two, and began a new journey, following the cries of my heart from one thing to another, searching out things that felt better and more authentic in my spirit than these. The more I saw of, and the more I got to know the outside world and all its violence and hatred, the more it appeared there was not even a God, or if there was a God, the punishing and hateful image of God must be true after all. Yet I still felt strongly in my heart that this was *not* the truth, and that this was not the whole of the world.

Then I found groups of people who were all about love and light and nonjudgment no matter what. Personal health and healing were of top importance, and supporting and being present for each other was encouraged as the highest good. God was labeled as *The Universe* here, and nothing punitive was ever threatened. These things felt much closer to the truth in my heart. I thrived there for a time, but I eventually began to realize many were using these things as a temporary bandage or a hiding place—pretending to heal and be healed in order to avoid truly facing their realities and experiences and... heal. Blind eyes were turned toward anything deemed too *dark* or *negative*, denying that parts of reality even existed, and therefore excusing themselves from ever taking any real action or responsibility—essentially putting their fingers in their ears and singing *La la la — I can't hear you!*

This light-and-fluffy community was still a bit lopsided.

I stopped being a part of anything then, and was just myself, taking care of my family and raising my children to be good people who were open and loving as best I could. I aimed to be the best father I could be from the heart-led awareness I had grown into, and this absolutely did not include a punishing God lurking around every corner.

Yet my Christian foundation never left me, and I was always aware that the culture around me was saturated with and based mostly on Protestant and Catholic Christianity. I realized that foreign religions and concepts that had helped and inspired my own growth so deeply were not always so insightful and helpful for everyone. I found most people were not open to strange and unfamiliar thoughts and imagery, and could not see past what was known and comfortable to them.

I had encountered a direct spiritual connection in other paths and experiences, and had learned to discern the energies of things outside myself or bigger than myself. I knew what *right* felt like and what *wrong* felt like—what was *light* and what was *dark*.

The Light I touched, encountered, and followed after was

eventually recognized to be what religions called God, and I was both surprised and delighted to find that this God was not the angry, hateful God, but a God who actually loved, actually cared, actually allowed people to be people—actually *connected* to people. In reaching out, searching for, and connecting with God for myself, I found no judgment, no criticism, no anger. The touch held nothing but peace, gentleness, and acceptance—nothing but love!

This was nothing like the God shown to me as a child.

As I began to realize that the only concept of God I had a problem with was the one with the image of the tyrant God, and that I actually *loved* this loving God I touched for myself, I reached the point I was able to begin re-immersing myself in the materials of my past. I began to retrace my childhood steps, searching the depths with a new light and understanding from the heart-led perspective. I also searched and felt into new materials that had been created in the fifteen years I'd been away from Christianity, to see what, if anything, had changed.

I found something I never noticed when I was younger: there seems to be two different Gods in Christianity. One God is found in the Old Testament of the Bible, and the other in the New Testament.

Although the old God does display some random acts of kindness and support, he is portrayed as mostly an angry, bossy God of vengeance and war. This is the God who hands down the list of rules to follow or die, as well as pages and pages and pages of exact specifications and commands for everything from building a tent to examining an infection—always with a *Do it right or die* insinuated, if not said right out.

But the new God is painted as an accepting and forgiving God who *does* go out of his way to show love to those who need it, who says all the rigid and legalistic rules are not what matters to be considered a good and worthy person, who seems to delight in overlooking offenses, and intentionally blesses those who do not deserve it.

This God feels so much more like the energy I felt for myself through direct connection!

The old God was demonstrated to the people by men who claimed to talk to and receive instructions directly from God, then told the people what to do based on this information. The new God was demonstrated by a man who claimed to be from a *direct connection* to God, then *showed* the people how to be, by living it himself. This struck me as a reflection of my own experiences of *being told by others* versus *connecting personally for myself*.

The God of the Old Testament breaks my heart. It has all the mentality and feeling of the *dark* energy I've felt other places and none of the *light* energy I've come to know. It disturbs me how *different* the two Gods are, and yet they are said to be the same God. We are taught that God never changes and is the same yesterday, today, and forever, but *how* can these two be the same? One tears down and confines, the other builds up and frees.

How was the old God ever one that people loved and followed, and still do today? Why is there such a huge focus on this patriarchal God with all his petty, immature, humanlike emotions, even here in the twenty-first century? It clearly fosters only hate, separation, and pain.

One obvious reason the old God is still fostered and kept in place is the control it gives those in power, those who have set themselves up as emissaries or mediators between God and others—classic bullying behavior. Step one, keep others disconnected and dependent on you for their information. Step two, instill a strong sense of fear of punishment and harm if the instructions are not followed. Step three, issue commands and control as desired.

But there is no fear in real love — love removes all fear!

This is not loving at all.

What is it people are hungry for? They are hungry for the new God — not because it is fluffier or all mushy lovey-dovey or allows them to get away with things they are guilty of and want to ignore or pretend like never happened, but because they are genuinely searching for *real* love. In their inner core, they know what unconditional love should be, they long for it and crave it with all they are. But where is their example of it in this world? Where is there any demonstration of this? Where is any hope shown?

This world is extremely punitive, and the image of the old God fits with and reinforces its agenda of power. Nearly every system is set up as a *succeed and earn what you deserve* or *fail and be punished* structure. Even parenting methods reflect this rewarding and punishing God, making it incredibly difficult for most people to be able to believe in the existence of a loving and compassionate God.

There are naturally so many human attributes pinned to the image of God, because we ourselves are human, and it is nearly impossible for our minds to imagine anything bigger or different than we are.

As I studied and read through the Bible's Old Testament for myself, looking for and feeling for answers to why the two Gods seem to be so different, I came to understand that maybe it is not God who was different back then and has now changed, but us. Maybe it has been our own growth over time, shifting our perceptions and the way *we* relate to God. Our history has many examples of progress and advances that evolved and developed over centuries of experience, increased knowledge, and new understandings. For example, the medical field especially has made massive improvements as we learn more and more about our own bodies and methods of treating them. Things like bloodletting and leeching and lobotomies are all considered archaic these days. We have also grown past primitive practices like hangings, or monarch rulers wielding absolute power, or believing the earth is the center of the universe with everything else orbiting around it.

What if God *has* always been the same, but the perception of the people back then was different, and their more primitive minds perceived what was bigger than they were as a more threatening predator to be appeased, just in case, to try to guarantee their safety? It may have been what they needed in that moment to survive and come together into a common community, and maybe they communicated and passed this information down the line to their children and grandchildren in the best way they knew how.

What if, when it came time for the old rules and portrayals to change, a movement naturally moved into play and began spreading—a movement of kindness and acceptance and the ability to connect to this thing bigger than themselves directly, without fear? What if one person ignited the spark of a different way of thinking, and what if that Way became a rolling snowball that gained momentum and slowly began to change the world?

In all this universe, the only constant and reliable thing is change. Everything has always changed, and will always change. If it has been the people who changed, and not the person of God who changed, then what could this mean?

God is not a person.

We are the people, surrounded by the air — the energy — of this *thing* we feel that is bigger than ourselves.

We can feel this bigger thing in sunrises and sunsets and forests and oceans and stars and in the eyes of our children and animals and acts of kindness and acts of forgiveness and acts of generosity and, when we are quiet and able to reach a peaceful state of mind, within our very selves.

When we touch this presence, no matter what we've done or what we find ourselves in the midst of, we are overcome with a sense of boundless peace, calmness, completeness, and... love. We become aware that our current problems, worries, and fears are not all there is. We feel a sense of a bigger picture, and can more easily see that all things are in constant motion, constantly changing. These things will pass.

If all these things are God, and this is all around us all the time, then why does the world around us seem to show more of the things that are *not* this love and peace? Why doesn't God just put an end to all the harmful things and make everything be this love that he is?

God is not a person.

God is an energy, a consciousness that we ourselves are made from and made of — hence, *made in the image of God*. We *are* this energy, and it is up to us to choose which God we wish to *be* in this world.

WRITING A BOOK ON God requires countless periods of stillness, feeling, prayer, and meditation to even know how to begin. This book has taken longer to write, and been the most difficult to write than any I've done before. I lost count of how many times I started over, searching for the right voice and tone it wanted. How can anyone describe such a thing? How can the right words be found to do justice to such an uncapturable topic? It is so vast and unexplainable that it can only be experienced directly. The Jewish culture respects this vastness so deeply they won't even speak it outside of reciting prayer, and will not spell the name out in writing — the closest they dare write it is G-d.

And yet, I have to. The need for this book has been in my heart, building pressure, increasing in demand for forty-one years now, and is at last being born — but it looks nothing like what I first felt and envisioned it would be.

When I first began collecting my thoughts and notes for this book, I had thought it was going to be a book about all the things that are wrong with religion. I had left the church fifteen years earlier and had spent that time exploring and experiencing many other paths and religions, and thought I was going to lay it all out straight for people once and for all.

Nearly a year into collecting my thoughts and notes for writing this book, I began attending a local church again — for the sake of my children, I claimed. The kids were twelve years old and five years old at the time, and had not grown up in the church, but had friends at school who talked about going to church. Though they had been raised with the morals one would learn in church, we decided it might be a good thing for all that to be reinforced and demonstrated through others who were not their parents, so we selected a church nearby that seemed to have potential and started attending.

As I immersed myself in the Christian community again, I began to notice... patterns? Synchronicities? Things within the church and its concepts I had previously had problems with that... actually made sense? I discovered that my years in other worlds had given me an understanding that could now look back at the Christian religion and understand what was going on, grasp what was really happening with all its symbolisms and rituals. All my training and practice in concepts of unity and oneness and of everything in existence being of the same energy was gradually revealed to have fallen short: I found I had apparently embraced everything as being one *except* the Christian path. This is ironic because one of the problems I had with the Christian church I knew growing up was its attitude that everything it taught was the *one* path, the only path, period.

I found the same shortfalls in my studies in compassion and love; residual anger and resentment toward Christians and the Christian community was slowly exposed within me, and needed to be dealt with and healed.

One of my Buddhist teachers, a nun named Namdrol, used to always stress to me the importance of community, of being a member of a group of other like-minded people. That had also been reiterated to me in various other books and magazines, as well as some of my own personal experiences. One article in particular imprinted my mind and heart with its emphasis that it was not *just* community that was important, but *our* community. It spoke of how the community and culture we were born into is most often the best place to find our enlightenment — and enlightenment *can* be found in each place and path. We don't have to adopt strange customs from other lands, or even travel to those other lands to learn any special tricks that are not already in our own backyard. At that time, I never dreamed I would set foot back in the Christian church, but now that article comes to mind years later, as I realize the truth of it.

I was born into the appropriate culture all along—I only needed the perspective of other cultures and concepts to turn lights on that truth.

And so, the intentions and purpose of this book shifted and evolved from being what is *wrong* with religion to what is *right* about religion.

But this was still not quite its final voice.

Something was still *off*.

Fast forward another few years, and I am found even more involved with the church and its studies and ministries, and am actually enjoying it. This book then became not even about what is *right* about religion, but simply about religion—or rather, the exploration of that which leads us to authentic connection with God, the intention of religion. This connection must be led by the heart, not by the mind. The mind tends to want inflexible, black-and-white concepts and rules, while the heart operates from a more fluidic and colorful palette of feeling and intuition.

Religion, in whatever path it is found, is simply a structure meant to guide toward larger truths and understandings. *Structure* is a scary word for many because it calls to mind the unbalanced way it is most often experienced: rigid and judgmental. The word *religion* itself is also a scary word because of the abuse of structure, and religion's association with it.

From the time we are born, we are bombarded with so much material and information—or misinformation—about God and spirituality that it's often very difficult to separate one thing from another and get down to the heart core of it. To reach the heart of it, we must connect to it for ourselves and let *it* tell *us* exactly what it is. We must find a way to throw out all teachings and all preconceptions of what we've been told the energy known as God is, and discover for ourselves what's still there. Zen Buddhism calls this *Shoshin*, or *Beginner's Mind*, the practice of always trying to approach a subject as if it were the first time we've ever heard it.

If we believe we've mastered a thing and can learn nothing more about it, we never will. If we believe there is always something new to learn about a thing — even when our degrees and educations declare we have now reached the top — and we are open to the possibility of tossing a piece or pieces of it out the window should new information be discovered or things prove to be different down the road, then we will always be able to see with fresh eyes, allowing the sacred space for growth to occur.

The practice of examining and re-examining our thoughts and beliefs, always open to greater depths and understanding, is absolutely essential for a healthy and balanced life.

Despite how deeply ingrained into our life we may feel something is, nothing is truly authentic or firmly rooted within us until it is our own deciding (our free will), and from our own determining (our experience): Do we believe what we believe and do what we do because it is our own conscious choice to do so? Because it is what feels right in our own heart? Or is it only because we were told it was right and what we should be doing?

Are we mind-led, or heart-led?

Religious and spiritual practice — our search for personal connection with that great, unexplainable, deep-and-wide energy that every being, whether human or not, senses — is one of the areas where the presence of the authentic, self-decided, and heart-led life is most important.

Yet religion is not the all-in-all of this — it's really only the starting point, the very first baby steps. Religion itself is not the goal; it is not the connection itself, but a prescribed or suggested set of signs pointing the way for you to find the connection for yourself.

Another popular saying goes *Do not mistake the finger for the moon*, meaning always seek out the heart of a matter — never assume the finger pointing the moon out to you *is* the moon itself. That is stopping too short, giving up too early, saying, *I know it all now.*

Look farther.

Dig deeper.

The most effective, most life-changing, most meaningful religion is the religion that fosters this personal connection mystically and directly to one's core — so much so that there is no separation between religion and life. At that point, it ceases to be religion — a tool — and simply becomes life: heart-led life lived from a flexible, unbreakable, and unshakable communion *with* God, the Great Connection.

To begin to discover the simple, bottom-line basis and purposes behind any given thing, whether that thing is religion or a clothes dryer, we must work our way backwards from the top, wading through all the moving parts that may have become complicated, miscommunicated, misunderstood, or distracting over time, until the basic components and solid footing of simplicity is revealed — the energy beneath it all.

And so, this book has now grown into becoming what it was titled all along, *The Energy of God.*

The voice it finally took on is in a style of talking for itself. My struggle was that my words and styles were never quite right for this work because it was not for me to write. Once I let go of all control and simply let the energy of God talk through me, everything clicked into place more powerfully than I could ever have created in a hundred billion years. I realized I cannot talk about God without being creative or artistic about it — without allowing space for the way the mystical is a free-flowing, fluidic form, because that is how I know God.

LMT
Spring 2019

If I speak with human eloquence
and angelic ecstasy
but don't love,

I'm nothing but the creaking of a rusty gate.

If I speak God's Word with power,
revealing all his mysteries
and making everything plain as day,
and if I have faith that says to a mountain,
"Jump,"
and it jumps,
but I don't love,

I'm nothing.

If I give everything I own to the poor
and even go to the stake to be burned as a martyr,
but I don't love,

I've gotten nowhere.

No matter what I say,
what I believe,
and what I do,

It means nothing without love.[4]

UNBOUND

WE ARE ALL GOD

OBSERVING THIS DAY AND age around us, I'm left speechless daily by the glaringly apparent ways we are complacently bombarded with violent images, surrounded with negativity, manipulated by our entertainment, and openly deceived by our leaders. When even the movements and revolutions that claim to be empowering people and bringing awareness and unity to certain areas are only thinly veiled permission slips to openly hate others and widen the imaginary gaps between *us* and *them* until it's not safe or okay to be *anything* anymore, it's clear something has gone terribly wrong. So many labels and non-labels have been created and applied and redefined and argued and fought for that I'm not sure anyone knows exactly what anything is anymore. What we're left with is a state of blind and chaotic confusion where everyone is extremely defensive and extra sensitive while trying their hardest to be just like everyone else, just like whatever the currently approved and popular thing happens to be—ironically screaming for their rights to be their own unique selves the whole time.

We're missing something.

Something is missing.

As I finally dive into writing the meat of this book that has simmered within me for over forty years, and taken shape within my notebooks for over four years now, we are currently approaching Holy Week in the Christian church: Palm Sunday, Maundy Thursday (or Holy Thursday), Good Friday, Easter Sunday. This time of year has always brought me to tears, whether I've been *with* the church in worship services and small groups or *apart* from the church in Buddhist services and pagan groups. Maybe it's the relief of winter finally turning to spring that makes me cry—the energy of new life and new beginnings. Maybe what makes me weep inside is that this time of year is always my birthday and I've somehow survived yet another spin around the sun. Or maybe it's the joy of many others feeling these same energies and joining together in a unity I've always known is possible—a unity I've always known is *meant* to be.

All these symbolize and embody what this holy week represents: love, life, liberation.

Wild love.

Unbound life.

Ecstatic liberation.

And these are pieces of the energy of God.

And these are the opposite of what these times have become.

There is a love that so desires others to be free from

suffering that it is willing to do whatever it takes for that freedom. This love is the mission of the Buddhist bodhisattvas, the actions of the Catholic saints, the selfless acts of countless heroes in myths and books and movies who help or save the lives of others, often at the cost of their own life or comfort. Whether you believe any of these people truly lived and did these things or if they are only stories meant to convey messages and inspirations does not matter. The messages and morals and symbols they carry *are* undeniably real and important to our daily lives as humans here. Images and symbols are key ingredients our human minds need to form our reality and process information.

In the imagery of this dramatic holy week, this love that works toward unity is exemplified by Yeshua: Jesus of Nazareth.

Yeshua, who was fully human and no different from any of us, was so in tune with his own essence and who he was, and so in communion with the environment and people around him that he felt and knew what results could come from loving others without reserve — what it *would* result in — and walked straight into it anyway. He allowed this love to so consume him that nothing else mattered. He taught by example, living the wild love, unbound life, and ecstatic freedom he knew is available and possible for everyone.

For centuries, the people and culture he was born into had been trapped in a system that, like our own times, left them blinded and in a state of chaotic confusion. This system taught the people they could do nothing for themselves except perform the extremely detailed rituals and exact procedures lined out for them — hollow rituals that were long outdated and extremely costly for families to keep up with. They were told they were bad people, that they were separated from God, and that God would be angry with and punish those who did not do these exact things the exact and correct way. On top of these, they had become increasingly persecuted and cramped by the Roman Empire occupying their lands. Love and unity were intentionally discouraged and squelched so those in control could *keep* their control and power.

Though there seemed no end to the growing darkness, their prophets and visionaries had promised them a revolutionary liberator would one day come and free them from oppression, and their hope for this was the only thing that kept them going as they longed for and dreamed of peace and safety.

Then, about three years before this holy week, they began to hear of a man traveling the area with an unconventional twist on their traditional teachings, and it was even said he had miraculous abilities like walking on water and healing all kinds of sickness and disease. They didn't know if any of these powers were true, and honestly didn't care whether they were literally true or not—their hopes were inflamed anew. This could finally be the one they had been waiting for! They could finally be getting their own kingdom back! Or maybe he was going to lead them to a new land where no one could bother them anymore! Or what if he was going to simply overthrow the Romans and take command himself right here in this place—a fair and just ruler at last!

When they heard that this man, Yeshua, was coming to their main city, Jerusalem, the people's excitement boiled over. They gathered together and swarmed the city entrance he was coming to, wanting to be a part of history, ready to be a part of the revolution—even ready to become an army for the liberator and fight if he asked them to. When they caught their first glimpse of him, he was not riding on a majestic war horse or arriving in a fancy chariot with an entourage, but was instead sitting on a simple young donkey. Amazed all the more by his humble simplicity, they shed their coats and robes and laid them across the road in front of him like a king's carpet, and those too poor for even a coat or a robe took palm leaves and laid them in the road. to give what they could for his cause. They sang and chanted. *Save us, Holy One! Help us! Blessed is the coming kingdom! Blessings to our king who has finally come!*

Yeshua watched all these things happening around him, feeling a mixture of overwhelming sadness and boundless love. As he listened to their words and felt their hearts, he knew they still misunderstood what his work was, what his message was about. He knew how easily swayed their desperate minds could be, tossed about by every wind and emotion. He had planted what seeds he could all around, and time was now quickly running out. He lovingly touched each outstretched hand as he passed by, and began to weep openly, saying, *If you only knew what it will take to bring you peace – but right now, it is hidden from your eyes...*

The people were focused on only the immediate physical things around them. They thought surely freedom would be in outward, physical form this way – a champion throwing off the chains of their abusers and oppressors. How else could change and liberation come? How else would the outcast and rejected people be accepted and allowed their own rights? They heard he had told one crowd that the kingdom of God was here, and they were ready to support Yeshua as the literal king of that kingdom. They had already convinced themselves he was coming to do away with the Romans. They expected it.

As I look around our present-day world, it seems that we,

too, shout and clamor for external, surface-level changes without examining anything deeper, without first acknowledging what is floating within. How much has *truly* changed with each switching of our leaders and politicians and in passing more and more laws and rules and restrictions in an effort to create change by sheer force alone?

No matter how often Yeshua had explained things to the people of his time, they still did not understand it was not a physical liberation he meant to set in motion. In both straightforward speech and in teachings wrapped in storytelling, he had made every effort to communicate deeper truths to people, to set them on the journey that would begin to open their eyes and minds. It was not the physical, outer ways of life and circumstances he worked to see changed, but the inward, personal ways of life. Yeshua understood that if a system was simply conquered by and replaced with another system, that would still be just another system, like only replacing one bad habit with another bad habit, leaving the internal motivations and influences untouched, unchanged. *Simply cleaning the outside of a cup does not clean the inside as well,* he told them, *but if you clean the inside of the cup first, then the outside will naturally be washed in the process. Then both the inside and the outside will be cleaned.* Surface changes and bandages were not what was needed to free them from suffering — nor is it what we need here and now.

It was these unfulfilled expectations and disappointed hopes that would drive these same people now calling for his crowning in joy to shout for his death in anger before the week was finished.

The way to bring about change is not to bash the undesired thing over the head to force it into a new shape. The most effective way to undermine an existing habit or system and begin a change is to dig to deeper and deeper levels — the root causes and influences that are driving and sustaining the system in the first place. Once these driving forces are unveiled, a remedy can then be intentionally applied to it, until it eventually replaces the undesired. This is how separation begins to be coaxed into connection.

What Yeshua taught was love, plain and simple. This was the kingdom of God he demonstrated. He knew that if the hearts of people could be softened and turned toward one another, the harmful problems that caused such separation would be realized and begin to naturally sort themselves out over time. He also knew he would not see immediate results; it would be an ongoing process over long periods of time.

When people are in the same boat, the differences between *you* and *me*, *us* and *them* begin to blur and disappear. The differences between *God* and *human* begin to blur and disappear. How can you harm someone you are face to face with on common ground? Yeshua taught that to love and protect others the way one would love and protect oneself or one's closest family members summed up all the hundreds of laws and rules and rituals they had been trying to live up to, to assure they were *good* people.

Though he did not agree with or approve of many of the circumstances of the time, it was ultimately not the physical suffering he aimed to change, but the suffering created by their separation from God, from each other — from love: the love that *is* God. The love that is *everything*. He knew if they could find and begin living as the boundless love that is the energy of God, their connection and unity with each other and all things would also be reestablished, saving them from the hell of the suffering they endured. Except in the case of *A Christmas Carol*'s Ebenezer Scrooge, change like this rarely happens immediately — it requires far-sighted effort and patience.

Yeshua did not recommend or direct anyone to rebel against the existing system; he only encouraged them toward love, kindness, and unity. Anything else would take care of itself. He knew love spreads, person by person, until it becomes an unshakable movement and begins to uproot the system from the inside out, like the washing of a cup.

As he passed through the crowds that Palm Sunday, the burden of love he felt for each person he saw, each pair of eyes he looked into, overwhelmed him to tears. Like holding on to a prophecy of hope, the desire to ease and help end their suffering is what kept him going, even though he knew what it would do to him.

He was here to be love in this place.

He was here to be God in this place.

He did not come to change the society or the religion — he participated in both completely. He did not intend to create a *new* religion, especially not one based on himself. He taught to clarify centuries of misunderstandings. He acted only to demonstrate and embody the energy of God in tangible ways that others could see, feel, and recognize in their own spirits as their own source of strength, to show that they, too, can carry it forward, embodying the energy in their own lives.

Some said Yeshua *was* God come into a body to be with us. Yet he was no more God than they themselves were.

Some said he was only a man, a carpenter who happened to have excellent speaking skills. Yet he was no more just a man than they themselves were.

Both of these mean the same thing: *we are all God.*

God *is* each of us.

As Yeshua entered the city that day, the leaders and those set in their ways grew frightened and tried to shut the people up, even saying directly to Yeshua, *Don't let them say these things! Tell them to be quiet!* They, too, had heard the stories of this man, and were afraid their worst nightmare was about to come true. Change would threaten their way of doing things, may prove they were not one hundred percent perfect, might diminish the authority and status they so enjoyed having. But he replied simply, *If we who are able to speak and act do not do so, and do not be the love of God in this place, then it will be left to these stones along the road to do.*

Love will always find a way to shine. If it is crushed in one place, it will rise in another, even if in a scattering of stones on the road.

Love never fails.

As our own society seems to have grown into a hollow, outdated system even beyond that of Yeshua's time, how can we merely sit by, complacent and silent? Are we satisfied with this state of things, as long as our own families have what they need? Is *us* and *them* comfortable enough that we can continue to ignore these things?

I could not avoid writing this book because the more I look around this world, what I see splashed across the headlines and posted throughout social media is the lack of God.

That lack of what God *is*.

We are here to be God in this place.

We are here to be love in this place.

I cannot say that I know God fully.
Nor can I say that I know God not.
The one who knows God best is the one who
understands the spirit of the words:
"Nor do I know that I know God not."

God the eye does not see
Nor the tongue express
Nor the mind grasp.
Different is God from the known,
And different is God from the unknown.

God is not the being who is worshiped of men.

So have we heard from the wise.[5]

L O V E

BRANCHES OF YOU

Sparrow was startled and took to the air as Monkey came crashing through the leaves. Landing high in a tree, she watched in wonder as Monkey frantically leaped from branch to branch, then dropped to the ground and began running in circles, flinging through piles of fallen leaves and sticks.

After a few minutes of watching, Sparrow finally called out, "Monkey! O Monkey! What are you doing down there?"

Monkey froze in his tracks and looked around wildly.

"Up here! It's Sparrow! What are you doing?"

"I can't see you, but I hear you. I'm looking for it!" He began scrambling around again.

"Monkey! What are you looking for?"

Never slowing this time, he called out, "Forest!"

"Forest?" asked Sparrow. "What is Forest?"

"Rattlesnake told me about it! He says it's the most beautiful

thing I'll ever see!"

"*It is? What does it do?"*

Monkey paused for half a moment before darting around again. "He said it's a perfectly perfect thing that can give anyone everything they could ever need — anything we can imagine!"

"*Wow, really?" asked Sparrow. "That sounds wonderful! He didn't say where it was?"*

"*No!" Monkey whined. "He slithered away lickety-split before I could ask, and I've been looking for it ever since! I have to find it now!"*

Sparrow thought about that. "How will you know when you find it?"

"*It will be* beautiful!*" Monkey cried as he poked his head into a fallen log.*

"*I want to see, too, then!" Sparrow began flitting about as fast as she could from branch to branch, ground to bush, stone to tree, looking for Forest. The more she looked, the more anxious she became. She flew faster and faster, feeling she could not relax until she, too, found the beautiful Forest.*

Higher and higher Sparrow went, leaving no tree unsearched as Monkey continued racing about below her.

When Sparrow broke through the treetops into the open sky, she proceeded to swoop back and forth, making wide arcs through the air. "Where, O where could it be?!" she moaned.

Suddenly, just as she turned back toward the trees she had emerged from, she gasped.

"*Monkey!" she called out. "Monkey! I've found it! I found the Forest!"*

Monkey could not hear her from so high up, so Sparrow went back down to where he was.

"*Monkey! I found the Forest!"*

"*What! You did? Where? Where is it? Tell me! I have to know! I have to go there* now!"

"*You're there!*" *Sparrow proclaimed.* "*These fruits, these trees, these bushes and stones and logs and branches and leaves — we've already been in the Forest the whole time!*"

WHEN YESHUA ENTERED JERUSALEM that day, the first thing he did was head to the temple, the sacred place specifically designated for the people to meet God. In addition to the long list of rituals and rules to live by that they were told guaranteed them God's good graces, they were told that it was here they could be in God's presence — that this was the *only* place they could meet God. God would not meet them just anywhere, especially if they were not one of the few deemed worthy to communicate with God — a priest.

One of the things the leaders were so threatened by was the way Yeshua's teachings contradicted this system. These leaders who felt so important and perfect in their own eyes were always trying to trick and trap Yeshua into breaking rules or speaking negatively about the system so they would have an excuse to take him away and settle back into their comfort zones. But Yeshua was too clever for that. Whether teaching crowds of people on hillsides or small groups of other teachers in the temples, he always managed to communicate his view and message without insulting the system right out. He taught against what he did not agree with by simply demonstrating and living its opposite, letting the harmful and corrupt things be exposed naturally in the contrast — a very effective sort of reverse teaching. Subtle, bold, and even sarcastic at times,

Yeshua proved himself to be a master teacher in these ways and many others, always able to meet his audience at whatever level they happened to be.

Though Yeshua went straight to the temple, he did not go to find God. He did not go to meet with God to find out what he needed to do next or to *check in* with God to make sure he was doing everything right or to *suck up* to God to make sure things would happen the way he wanted them to happen. He understood God was all around, all the time. He talked to and heard from God constantly, wherever he was. He knew every*thing*, every*where*, and every*one* was God. He taught his followers and the crowds of people that came to hear him that no one has to go looking for God — that is pointless and even a bit ridiculous, like a fish trying to find the ocean, like a sparrow trying to find the forest: they're inside the thing they're searching for all along. They can't get away from it.

But he compassionately understood the people did not know this, did not understand they were already surrounded by and already a part of the energy of God, even as they went about their chores and errands each day and weren't specifically thinking about God. I'm afraid we are no different in our own age of endless entertainment, technology, and distractions.

The temple was formed to be a symbol of bringing people together where they can physically see the unity they *are*, the sameness of purpose they share, and the community they are meant to be. The temple is meant to be a place where love is communicated; love is meant to be realized as everything — the all in all.

Yeshua also understood the nature of the mind to wander all over the place like a frantic monkey, and he knew the value of symbols and rituals as tools to help the mind focus. The temple or church or mosque is not meant to only be a place to literally meet God and each other, but a place to focus, reflect, and become *aware* of God and each other, aware of who and what God *is*, all around.

The ancient Celtic Christians had a practice called *caim* prayers, or circle prayers. In this practice, the people would draw or make the motion of a circle around themselves as they recited prayers of God's presence and protection. But they did not believe it was this encircling ritual itself that protected them or think that God *needed* them to do this in order to come be with them. The Celtic people knew God was already around them, already protecting them. They practiced this ritual solely for the sake of their own minds. It was an action to bring their own attention to the facts that already existed, to focus their awareness on the energy of God they knew was *already* present. Here, they became aware that *they* were in *God's* presence, reminding their forgetful and distracted minds.

Members of the Roman Catholic church and other liturgical churches cross themselves in this same way, making the sign of the cross on themselves by drawing with their fingers from forehead to chest and shoulder to shoulder as blessing or protection. They know the sign itself does nothing, but the awareness of mind it brings of God's presence serves to strengthen and reassure the one performing the ritual. Any type of prayer functions in these ways; it is an action that brings the focus and reminder of, *Oh yeah, I remember there is a bigger picture here – I am a piece of things bigger than myself.*

I believe Yeshua went directly to the temple that day to see how well the people were finding God in this symbolic place, the sanctuary of the capital city, the only starting place a person could begin trying to figure out what God *is* for themselves. He knew the system had become a tool designed to keep them at a distance — that was a big part of what he aimed to change — but despite that, he still held hope there were those who sincerely tried to find God even through these difficulties.

Already in a deeply saddened and distressed mood from his entrance into the city and his inner emotions surrounding the things he knew were looming closer, what he found when he entered the courtyard of the temple walls sent him over the edge. Tables and booths had been set up all around the entrance, and businessmen were selling the cattle, sheep, and doves the people needed to bring as the sacrifices for their required rituals — animals and materials that were supposed to be from their own belongings, offered to God from their own lives! Moneylenders had also set up tables to exchange the traveler's foreign currency to the local currency, dishonestly swindling the pilgrims who were unaware of the correct exchange rates. All around, they were blatantly taking advantage of the people, not even trying to be subtle in their manipulation — and this was being allowed!

Overcome with despair and filled with anger, Yeshua made a whip and began driving the salespeople out of the temple, flipping over their tables, sending their money rolling across the courtyard, and herding the animals out into the streets, roaring, *Stop this! Get out of here! This is supposed to be the house of God, a house of prayer for all the world, a place of safety and trust – and you have turned it into a bloody den of thieves and robbers?! Get. OUT!!*

I wonder what those who had followed him from the city gates thought at these things. Maybe some were frightened and left, turned off at the disappearance of his gentle manner. Maybe others threw their fist in the air, let out a whoop, and joined him in smashing tables. Maybe some stood frozen, staring in shock at the utter *human*-ness being shown by this man who was supposed to be God in flesh. He had stopped and taken the time to *make* a whip. He was intentional and fully aware of what he was doing.

Was this love?

If Yeshua's purpose on earth was to show others how to love again, destroying property and screaming at people seems to be the opposite of this. Isn't love supposed to be calm and gentle and the repeated overlooking of every offense, taking everything that happens to it with a big smile? What happened to all his previous examples of hanging out with outcasts and defending those who were considered untouchable by all society? What about accepting people just as they are? These simple business people were only trying to make a living for themselves, weren't they?

One of my favorite Buddhist bodhisattvas is named Manjushri. A bodhisattva is one who devotes their life to serving and loving others, and commits to always be a benefit to others in every conceivable way. Manjushri holds a long, fiery sword over his head, and one of the lines of his mantra says *With your flaming sword of wisdom you are quick to cut down all roots of suffering wherever they begin to appear.* Manjushri with his sword is a powerful reminder that love is not only sweet, unconditional acceptance of all things as they are, but also vigilant, mindful alertness watching both self and others for anything that will harm and separate from love and unity— then having the courage, wisdom, and discernment to take whatever action is needed to remedy and heal the situation.

The salesmen and moneychangers who had set up shop for their own profit in the temple were adding to the system that kept the people bogged down in the physical world only, blinding the eyes of the people and keeping them distracted, keeping them focused on surface rules and regulations, keeping them from discovering that everything around them is also God. The business people themselves probably didn't even realize the roles they were playing, didn't realize the harm they were causing. An enraged Yeshua took up his flaming sword of love and proceeded to cut down this root of suffering and persecution and division. He taught his followers, *Things that cause people to stumble are bound to happen in life, but there will be tremendous sorrow for the ones who cause this stumbling — it would be better for them to be thrown into the sea with a large stone tied around them.*

Yeshua was not saying these people were worthless and better off dead, nor was he endorsing a death penalty; he was giving a comparison image that to be trapped under water unable to breathe or swim up for air would still be less miserable than the type of energy these people who were profiting dishonestly off others were going to bring back onto themselves. By driving them out of the courtyard, Yeshua *was* loving the business people as well as their victims. He saw the bigger picture, all around. The same actions that manifested for defending one side also manifested as *tough love* to the other side, but it was all love. Yeshua took action for the benefit of all sides, putting a stop to one side from further harming themselves and others, and putting a stop to the other side from being harmed.

I do not recommend anyone try to make an overall judgment and take such drastic action as Yeshua did in this story though — there is no way anyone can know every detail of a situation or what another person has been through. We clearly have the responsibility to help protect and stand up for those in need when we become aware of an opportunity to do so, but there is no way we can act as judge, jury, and executioner in *any* situation. This would be the height of arrogance, and far from serving others.

Sometimes love is tough—tough to give, and tough to receive.

How do we love that unpleasant person who is negative about everything and cuts down every comment or idea, or that horrible bully who is unapologetically hateful and violent toward other fellow humans, or that self-centered family member who only drains and leeches everyone around them?

How do we receive the correction and instruction offered to us by those who love and care about us? How do we accept love that is shown to us in areas we feel unworthy or unlovable or not good enough in? How can we believe a certain love is truly unconditional when so much of this rewards-and-punishments world around us is extremely conditional?

Love is not some nebulous cloud drifting around aimlessly and if we happen to walk through it, *Boom!* we found love. Love is a verb, as the old saying goes. Love requires action. Love requires a conduit, a channel. Where are these channels going to come from? How will these channels manifest in this place, in these days?

When someone is in need, does the energy of God manifest before them suddenly in some sort of bodily form and meet their need on the spot, or does someone or some thing happen to match up in perfect timing to help, turning out to be exactly what was needed in the nick of time?

These channels are found in our own hands, in our own feet.

We are the temple.

We are the church.

We are God, all around.

And we can't give what we don't have—you can give love because you *are* love; you can receive love because you *are* love.

Yeshua did not believe God was found in only one place and only through certain people. He demonstrated this to those who gathered to listen to him by saying, *The Kingdom of God (or the Kingdom of Heaven) is in the humble ones. Those of the Kingdom of God comfort those who suffer and grieve. The Kingdom of God is with the gentle ones. Those of the Kingdom of God advocate for equality and justice. The Kingdom of God seeks and fosters compassion. Those of the Kingdom of God desire to uplift and encourage. The Kingdom of God desires peace and unity. Those of the Kingdom of God are committed and trustworthy, determined and steadfast no matter what others may do to them.*

All these describe acts and qualities of love.

The Kingdom of God is love.

The energy of God is love.

God is love.

One time the leaders tried to trick Yeshua by asking him when the Kingdom of God would come. Yeshua replied, *The Kingdom of God is not something that can be observed. It is not any one thing that can be pointed to. No one will ever be able to say definitively "Here it is," or "There it is," or "This is what it is," because the Kingdom of God is within you.* He expounded on this further to his followers later, saying, *Even I cannot fully represent the Kingdom of God to you, for, like you, my life is but a momentary flash of lightning that lights the sky from one side to the other, and then is gone again. Those who call out "Here he is," or "There he is," surely do catch a glimpse of me, but do not go running after them; it will be gone once again. Instead, find me for yourselves, and rivers of living water will flow from within you. You cannot rely on me alone; the kingdom of God is within you. The love I have demonstrated for you is like the vine, and you are like branches of that vine, spreading throughout the earth.*

I can imagine this threw them for quite a loop, as these people had up and left their jobs and families and everything they had to follow and learn from him. He was their guru. What would they do if they didn't have him to teach and explain things to them?

To love without agenda was the totality of his message. *Whenever you welcome another person in love, you are welcoming me; and whoever welcomes me does not welcome me but welcomes the one who I represent,* he said. *Whenever you treat any thing, any plant, any animal with honor and respect and love, you are honoring and respecting and loving God.*

What would this world begin to become if everyone chose to treat everyone and everything as if it were God?

No one knows all the qualities of God fully, but we can recognize and know love when we see it—we see it in each other.

And love can be here any time *we* choose.

Every time we choose.

It's all up to us.

My life blazed with the desire
To serve as a thread
Joining the heaven and Earth[6]

CREATION

MOUNTAINS IN THE SEA

YESTERDAY I STEPPED OUTSIDE to stand on the grass in my bare feet. I love the feel of nothing between my skin and the earth, the direct connection to our home here. Doing this has always felt like a long exhale to me, the energy flowing over me and through me as a soothing waterfall, allowing me to relax and let go of all the daily worries and demands that stack up on my shoulders. I begin to remember there are things bigger than myself and my problems, and start to realize that I might not have to save the entire universe all on my own today after all.

It might seem that thinking about how small I and my worries are compared to the larger planet and even greater cosmos would make me even more anxious and stressed out, make me feel even more insignificant and unable to handle the things that may be worrying or upsetting me in the moment, but it's actually the opposite that occurs. Instead, I feel the tension begin to ease. I can relax and take a deep breath. I can let go of trying to control everything.

But if I am such a tiny little being in such a vast universe full of the unknown, shouldn't I be constantly afraid I may be crushed and snuffed out of existence at any moment? Don't I *need* to control everything I can and make sure nothing *out there* can come *in here* and make something happen I don't want to happen? How can I be feeling *more* secure in this perspective?

The difference is that one of these is operating from a place of connection, and the other from a place of separation.

After many years and much trial-and-error, I've found the key that makes the difference between the restlessness and the restfulness is in realizing and touching the awareness that the vastness *out there* is not separate from myself at all. It is not actually *out there* but *right here*—or it is not *only* out there but *also* right here. I am a *part* of this largeness and not some puny *other* thing getting bounced around as if trapped inside a cosmic pinball machine. There is no *me* and *not-me*, no *self* and *other*. There is only *everything*. Us.

I know I'm made from the same stuff as everything I see and experience around me because once I set aside all distractions and be still, I know. I *feel* it. This could be described with imagery saying that I'm feeling how I'm a valid part of God's creation and have been spoken into existence the same way everything else has been, or it can be described in ways that say I'm realizing I'm one with the universe and therefore seen and known—I am not abandoned.

However one chooses to visualize these, once one realizes this truth, the worries stacked on one's shoulders always turn out to be just a simple game of Jenga tiles: when enough of the pieces are pulled out of the stack, the whole tower comes crashing down.

This *stuff* you and I and everything around us are made of is energy. We are formed from the same energy everything else that has ever existed has been made of, and we are currently holding the energy that will make up everything *after* us. We are the image of all that was, and all that is, and all that is to come. The ancient Hindu text known as the *Ashtavakra Gita* or *Song of Ashtavakra* beautifully reminds us of this circle of life by simply saying, *All things naturally arise, rush against each other playfully, and then subside.* The *Tibetan Book of the Dead* explains that when one recognizes they are the same as the light, the All, they become free. The Christian Bible tells us we were made in the image of God, that God was before all things and is the substance that holds all things together, and that God is over all and through all—that God *is* all and is *in* all. Even science has discovered that at quantum levels there is no such thing as separation, that everything truly is connected to and influenced by everything else, regardless of distance.

All paths and cultures have their own local words and images to explain how everyone and everything is literally everything and everyone. All that is, is God, and we cannot even begin to fathom every aspect of every angle and every experience of the energy of God—of what we *all* are.

On many layers we are literally God walking the face of the earth, here and now.

One of the men in Yeshua's immediate circle of friends, John, began his written account of Yeshua's story by saying *In the beginning was the word, and the word was with God, and the word was God.* The original Greek of this word *word* John uses is *logos*, which simultaneously means both the speaking and the thought behind the speaking. It is the will to create, the act of creating, and the creation itself, all at once, just as an artist pours herself into her work, and her art is an expression of herself — she is at once the artist and the art. We are at once the art and the artist. With every word we choose to speak and every action we choose to take, we are presenting God to others, who are also God. We are God painting pictures for God, who paints pictures of God for God. Who knows what image or angle or way God will take on for us next?

We are all the image of God, the image of the energy of All That Is.

One of the most fascinating things about life on this earth is the way the same thing can be a different thing to a different person, or a different image from a different angle. I can simultaneously be a friend to some, a stranger to others, a lover, an enemy, a father, a son, a brother, a co-worker, or a former co-worker — but I'm still just one person, still only me. Looking even deeper reveals further layers and I can see some of my friends know of my artistic side while others have no clue I have ever done anything artistic. My fellow employees know me one way, but not all of them know of my inner thoughts and beliefs or that I also have a rich, life-long spiritual life that encompasses multiple cultures and pathways beyond my work and office personality. My children know me as their dad and know a bit of how I see the world as I show it to them and teach them about it, but I hope one day down the road they come to know even more about me and my life as a person no different than they are, and how I came to be this person I am. That's something I now wish I had had the opportunity to learn about my own ancestors.

No matter how close we are to someone, we are still only ever seeing a tiny clip of that person. Each person has been through more experiences than anyone can count, on more layers than anyone can count. Each experience has interacted with their unique chemistry and makeup and shaped their thought patterns and view of the world over long periods of time. Some external experiences beyond their control have even affected them physically, emotionally, and mentally, whether traumatically or positively. Each thought pattern and world view causes them to respond to each new thing or person they encounter in instinctual, often subconscious ways.

There is no way to know all that another person has been through to cause their actions or appearances as we observe them in the present moment. The man on the street corner holding a cardboard sign, the kids whose clothes look like they are hand-me-downs two sizes too small, the woman in the grocery store who breaks down in a panic attack for seemingly no apparent reason. What right do we have to judge another person at a glance based on a momentary appearance?

In attempts to feel more secure, we try to fit people into exact little boxes, perfect little descriptions to summarize miles of personal experience they have lived. We need to control everything around us, and we need things to have definite and permanent answers. But like trying to understand every aspect and incarnation of the energy of God, life as a human is far more complicated and complex than any single black-and-white definitive statement can cover.

The more we spend time with somebody or something, the more we begin to see and know them; further layers begin appearing to our awareness like magic. When I was barefoot in the grass of my backyard, I was at first aware of only the superficial layer of things: trees, grass, dirt, fence, neighbor's house, fresh air, breeze on my skin, sun on my face. But then, the longer I stood there quietly observing, the more things and details I began to see all around me: robins, blue jays, cardinals, and mockingbirds flitting among the branches of the trees, a squirrel trying to remember where he buried his treasure in the shadows of the trees, an abandoned cicada skin clinging to the post of the porch, a beetle traveling in and out of view along the grass to who knows where, the way the tree branches clearly don't like the electricity of the power lines and grew themselves around the wires to avoid it, how old and tall and strong the middle tree is compared to the others around it, the unexpected direction the clouds are floating which is not the direction the wind is blowing my hair down here on the ground — all of these were present all along, though they seemed to appear out of nowhere, like magic to my mind.

We never see everything at once. Our first look really reveals only a broad, generalized overview of a thing. Our minds observe as big a picture as it can before anything else, scanning widely and taking in as much as possible, ignoring finer details — a survival trait embedded in us to bring awareness of what's going on all the way around us. That's simply how our human mind naturally operates. Then, if we remain in that place and keep looking, keep watching, we begin to see other details emerge we hadn't noticed before.

This is what Yeshua does in story after story about him. He never takes anyone at face value or judges them on how they happen to appear in the moment as the leaders and teachers who thought themselves perfect did. The practice of these teachers was to reject and shun entire lists of people based on a few quick facts about them — sometimes as little as a single assumption or rumor. They were even quick to cast out their own peers if they seemed to not follow the same ways they themselves did or began to question things too much, so when they saw Yeshua, who was in this circle of teachers, not only interacting with people on these lists but actually going to their houses and spending quality time with them, they were shocked and enraged.

As a human, Yeshua saw only other humans, not lists of the traitors and the faithful or the approved and the disapproved. He looked beyond the surface appearances and searched for the heart of everyone he encountered, knowing each person has value and holds the same breath of life everyone and everything else has. No one is unworthy. Everyone has the potential to connect to life and end all separation and suffering; no color, religion, gender, or status is ever a problem blocking this freedom.

And this is love.

The daily life and humanness of Yeshua is an aspect that is often overlooked or even completely disregarded in the light of him being considered to be God in flesh. Focusing only on this dazzling aspect paints him as a glowing ethereal figure who mysteriously lived among us for thirty-three years over two thousand years ago, and that shiny image is what is portrayed as The Model we should all act like if we are good people at all. Like the people of Yeshua's time, we are told that if we are not these perfect things, we are separated from God and will be cut off and thrown out. If we are not good enough and don't earn our place, it's out the door with us—and we can forget about being representatives of the energy of God here. One slip and everything we've ever done is discredited and worthless.

But who can measure up to such a dazzling and perfect mold, especially in these human bodies with all their complicated chemicals and messy emotions? How can we be expected to so perfectly be this type of God here? How can we stop being human when we're human? How do we get from here to there? Where do we even start to begin changing the naturally human things about ourselves into the prescribed and approved character of God?

Maybe we don't have to.

Maybe we aren't supposed to.

It's impossible, no matter how hard we try, and this list is no different that the approval lists the leaders and teachers of Yeshua's time tried to enforce.

The temper tantrum Yeshua threw in the temple shows just how human he is, and smashing tables wasn't the only very human thing Yeshua did in his life. Many examples are scattered throughout his stories. In one version, after visiting the temple and driving all the business people out of the courtyard, he and his followers started toward the edge of the city where they were going to spend the night. Yeshua felt hungry and saw a fig tree off to the side, but when he reached it, found it had produced no fruit to eat. It was not the season for fruit to be on the trees, so nobody expected there to be. His followers were then caught off guard when in frustration, he spat, *Curses on you! May you never bear fruit again!* At that, the tree instantly withered and died.

There are layers of reasons why he did this. One reason was to show us the irrational levels our human emotions and chemicals can steer us. If it wasn't the season for fruit, why would Yeshua expect there to be fruit? And does because it wasn't the season for fruit give him any right to get angry and curse the tree? Yet we do unreasonable things in the same ways, lost inside storms of emotion swirling within us. Seeing an example of such actions outside ourselves is one way to possibly spark recognition of any sort of lack of discipline we may have ourselves. Once we recognize and acknowledge something unreasonable we'd like to change in ourselves, we can begin to consciously work on changing it.

When his followers gathered enough courage to ask him about his reaction with the fig tree, he gave them a discourse on how the energy behind our words and intentions can move mountains into the sea. Everything we do matters. Everything we do affects everything else on some level. We are all a part of the same whole, and when we harm another, we harm ourselves. This fig tree demonstration was to warn us to be very careful with our actions and words; they have effects — sometimes very harmful ones.

We are mountains rising from the sea.

We are lights on hills, seen by everyone all around, influencing others whether we are aware of it or not.

We are artists painting the world and image of God around us. What sort of painting do we want to create? We hold the brush in our hand.

But it's not about *becoming* anything at all. It's simply about taking a look at ourselves and consciously choosing what sort of person we are going to be, and then taking a look at the immediate world around us and choosing what sort of person we are going to be to them, what sort of energy we are going to put out into the world, what angle we are going to embody to others and for others. We already have all we need for this; we are already what we want to be.

One thing Yeshua did encourage us to be unreasonable with is loving. Love is the only thing we are told to be irrational in.

Don't try to be Yeshua.

Don't try to be God.

Just try to be love, in every situation.

Love wildly.

Love first, ask questions later.

We choose the energy of God. Our thoughts and actions have power.

Which God will we portray: a loving God, or a hateful God?

It is for freedom that
the energy of God has set us free.

Stand firm, then,
and do not let yourselves be burdened again
by the enslaving ties of separation and division.

You, my brothers and sisters,
were called to be free.
But do not use your freedom to chase after things
that are temporary and fleeting;

instead, care for one another humbly
in love,

for the entire message is fulfilled
in following
this one instruction:

Love everyone.[7]

IMAGE

FACE TO FACE

I'VE ALWAYS BEEN FAR more influenced by the human Yeshua than the godman Yeshua, and the way the two are often spoken of together forms an impossible conception that unfortunately only inspires and reinforces feelings of unworthiness and failure for most people. When presented to us as a tangible example of how the energy of God can be in this place, these two conflicting Yeshuas can be very confusing.

On one hand, we are told Yeshua was completely God come down to become a human among us, yet still did everything absolutely perfectly, without error—as flawless as God is supposed to be. He is assumed to have entered this plane with full awareness that he was God, even as an infant. On the other hand, we are told he was also completely human and experienced absolutely everything in life on earth the same way we do.

But as humans, we are messy and complicated, tossed about by the chemicals and emotions in our minds and by the biological functions built in to our systems that launch us into autopilot modes that are so difficult to control at times. None of these are new to our modern times; all ancient stories and myths that still exist reveal that as long as humans have been on this planet, this is how things have been. If Yeshua experienced everything we experience, then he also went through all these. If Yeshua was never affected by the struggles and learning curves that are a part of life as a human, he was not human.

When it's talked about how God became a human, became one of us, it's most often in a negative connotation toward ourselves, insinuating our complete unworthiness: *we poor, pathetic, weakling humans down here needed such help that Yeshua had to come and experience how miserable it is to be human himself, to both get our attention and to finally show us how we are supposed to be.*

This guilt-trip inspiration is supposed to uplift and encourage us toward goodness?

Humanity is not all struggles and learning curves by any means. Humans also experience so many beautiful things, which means that human Yeshua also found and experienced these things of beauty. We clearly see this in what he chose to center his teaching on; he encouraged those who listened toward the beauty that is always present even in the midst of suffering.

Sadly, our world today seems to downplay Yeshua being human and instead places much more emphasis on Yeshua literally being God. The focus on the godman is meant to impress to us and display to us an ultimate authority figure we dare not contradict, and what focus *is* on the human Yeshua is meant to convince us that he also personally knows and understands the human condition—our feelings and experiences—and is therefore fully trustable as the godman to obey. The God is meant to inspire obedience; the man is meant to demonstrate our capability to do what is expected of us and from us. In this, we receive the strong suggestion that we must be as perfect as Yeshua if we are to be considered good enough to be associated with him and an official member of the kingdom he spoke of. We get the message that to be human is to be flawed, and to be perfect is the proper way, the holy way.

How convenient this fits right in with the social pressures and expectations placed on us in this world: Be perfect or be worthless. Be the right color or be abused. Believe the right things or be killed.

When presented to us in this way, this imagery is not an uplifting encouragement, but another tool of manipulation, designed to perpetuate a stifling of love and to foster feelings of unworthiness which can then be further manipulated and controlled.

So we have the picture painted for us that after watching us from somewhere above for thousands of years, God finally decided to come down and become one of us, to see just what it was like to be human and show us how perfect we're supposed to be. But where is the humanity in a perfect God-person image? Where is the perfection and so-called godliness in a human example? It's clear that the *fully God yet fully human* as it is portrayed this way takes pieces of the reality but misses the mark of its true meaning.

Yeshua was indeed fully God and fully human, but being perfect had nothing to do with it. Godliness does not mean perfectness, just as humanness does not mean being flawed.

Yeshua was fully human and fully God the same way we are all the human embodiments of God on this level of physical reality. The very idea that God is *somewhere above* while we are stuck down here below creates an instant separation, the feeling of an unreachably distant energy we can never hope to cross. Yeshua found and touched that energy, discovered that the energy *was* himself, and saw that every single other person was *also* himself, also the same energy. His mission became to show us how to cross this imaginary distance—even though it would bring him to an abrupt end at another kind of cross!

This is the kingdom he illustrated to the people in both stories and actions. This is the love he found and could not be all right with keeping to himself. He *had* to spread it around. He *could not* remain silent amid cruelty, judgment, and discrimination. Even in the traps and mind games the leaders tried to set for him to discredit and eliminate him, he was able to pinpoint the most loving response, oftentimes turning the trap backwards on to those setting it.

Is there any difference in the cruelty, judgment, and discrimination we are surrounded by in this world today? Where is the Yeshua to demonstrate the most loving way today? Who will be his hands, his feet, his voice here and now?

One time, after discussing and grumbling together about the way Yeshua was so lenient, forgiving, and accepting of people who had done things they considered to be clearly wrong, the leaders grabbed a woman and brought her to him. *Great Teacher,* they said mockingly, *This woman has been accused of sleeping with someone other than her husband. You know the laws we all follow command that such a woman be put to death by throwing rocks at her, but what do* you *say about this?* Yeshua looked at the woman, then looked to the men accusing her, turned his back to them, sat on the ground, and silently began to write in the dirt with his finger. *Hello! Teacher! We asked you, what do you say should be done about this wicked woman?* they prodded as he continued to remain silent. *Answer us! Do you say we should follow the law or break it?* Yeshua slowly stood back up then, looked at them, and answered, *Do whatever you are going to do, but let the one who has never done anything wrong throw the first stone at her.* Then he sat back in the dirt and began writing once again. As the minutes went by after that, the accusers began to melt back into the crowd one by one, until every one of them had gone. They had set what they thought was a foolproof trap: if Yeshua said to let the woman go, he would be proven to be a lawbreaker and they would have their case against him, but if he agreed with them and condoned the woman's death then all his previous actions and messages on love and mercy would be discredited and as the news of this hypocrisy spread, he would no longer be a threat to their power over the people.

Instead, Yeshua assumed the most humble position he could, sitting in the dirt, and allowed the moment to linger, giving both the accusers and the crowd time to think about what was happening here. This in itself is an example of a practice that applies to everything everywhere, even to us today. If we can find the space to wait a while — even just the space of only a few minutes — whenever we are pressed with a decision, or feeling the urge toward a spur-of-the-moment reaction, it can allow clarity and fresh air into the situation. It can allow the breath of life to flow between and among the situation, and allow reality to set in, which is often different than our emotionally-colored minds can realize at the same instant the thing is happening. If we can accomplish this momentary pause, we will then find ourselves much more open to finding and receiving a solution that may present itself.

As Yeshua waited the situation out, perhaps he was writing out a list of other laws they were supposed to be following, knowing that they had most likely broken them at some point in their own lives. Maybe he was writing the names of each accuser themselves, demonstrating that they were not as safely anonymous as they may have felt. Or maybe he was simply writing *Love everyone* over and over.

Whatever he was writing in the dirt, when he stopped and looked up again, he found only the woman standing there. *Where did they go? Did none of them condemn you?* he asked. *No one, sir,* she replied. Yeshua smiled at her then. *Then neither do I. Go home, and be love.*

Every example and story we have demonstrates that to be godly is simply to love — how did the idea that godliness equals perfection even come about? Every illustration shows that God is only the love that everything is created of, including ourselves — love that loves no matter who, no matter what.

That sort of love *is* perfect, choosing to love the way the sun shines on both the good and bad without judgment, the way the rain falls on both the kind and unkind without condition.

This is the sort of love that changes lives. I believe the woman Yeshua refused to condemn that day was the woman we know as Mary of Magdala — Mary the Magdalene — and that the love he demonstrated to her, her accusers, and the entire crowd that had gathered *did* change her life forever. Whatever harmfulness she had gotten herself into that had landed her in that situation to begin with apparently did stop because we see her again later at home with her sister and brother, Martha and Lazarus, lovingly and devotedly participating in the family and in the community when Yeshua comes to visit them.

If Yeshua is the physical example for us of the energy of God, then to be godly is clearly to be loving, compassionate, and kind. Because God is everything, everywhere, in every way, on every layer, it is extremely difficult to describe and pinpoint a definite description beyond these things, beyond *act fairly, love kindness*, and *walk humbly*. Even the most poetic languages and most abstract concepts fall vastly short of encompassing this energy.

The only way our human minds are able to conceptualize and attempt to understand things is to create imagery, visuals, and stories around things — to put a face on it. This is the way we communicate to each other and pass information down to following generations. This is the purpose and need for rituals, ceremonies, and symbols like the symbol of the temple. This is where the hundreds of faces of deities and gods and demons in every culture from the Hindus to the Greeks came from: each characteristic in life and every emotion experienced was given a face and a name. This provided a way to communicate and express more subtle things with each other, as well as a way for our own minds to process our experiences and aspirations. Yet every culture has always understood and known that all the faces are really only one face, only one energy with different hats, the same way one person can be a daughter and a mother and a sister all at once, yet still only one person. It is only our *modern* society that cannot seem to understand the concept and importance of multiple faces. Current western society insists there is only one specific, perfect, old-man-in-the-sky type of God character.

From the first appearance of humans on this planet, we have felt a connection to something bigger. The imagery of God has emerged to embody this feeling and help the human mind connect to it, but the image of the perfect God to be measured against, with condemnation and discrimination given to those who fall short of this unrealistic perfection is extremely harmful in every way. This type of God comes with a list of rules, do-and-don'ts, and criticisms, saying if you fail to follow all these exactly and perfectly, you're out — rejected.

Who can live up to that?

The idea that Yeshua was perfect comes from the way he was described as *without sin*. A misunderstanding of what sin is causes the misunderstanding and assumption that Yeshua was perfect, which in turn causes the further conclusion and expectation that we, too, must then be perfect.

Sin is commonly portrayed as being a disobedience, a criminal offense, or a rebellion. We're told we are naturally sinful, bad, and wrong. We're told that we were born this way without option, and are therefore essentially a horror to God simply for existing — even though God is supposedly also the one who intentionally and consciously made each and every one of us. Then we are told that Yeshua was without sin, as proof to us just how hopelessly horrible we are in contrast. We are given a long list of things to avoid doing so that we are not *living in sin*, so that God will be able to notice us and give us things we want — a full circle return to the exact situation the people in Yeshua's time were dealing with.

Sin has continued to be a definition for people themselves, basically a nametag reminding themselves and everyone around *Hello, My Name is Not-Yeshua*.

But *sin* is only another word for *separation*.

If I choose to speak loudly in the public library and get myself thrown out and banned from returning, I've been separated from the library — I've been blocked. If I'm holding my car keys in my hand and I allow something to make me so angry I just throw whatever is in my hand or within reach, and my keys end up lost in the bushes somewhere, I've then become incapable of entering or driving my car, I've been separated from my vehicle and everywhere I needed to go and everyone I needed to be with. If, in the course of my day, I choose an action that is not the most loving action possible for that moment, I then become apart from love — apart from God — in that moment, as well as distant and disconnected from the person or thing I was just unloving toward. I am separated.

Some things on the list of sins are things that can cause our separation from the love that God is, a separation from the love that *we* can be in this place — not because of the thing itself, but because of the disconnect it creates in its opposition to what love is. It forms a chasm between what we chose to become in that moment and the love we could have been.

When it is said that Yeshua was without sin, it means Yeshua was without separation, without disconnection. He was vividly aware of the energy of God in every moment as he went through his daily life and all its struggles. In all the ups and downs of messy human life, he never lost sight of the love that created all things, and was therefore in tune with God as well as with everyone and everything around him.

Two sides of a double-edged sword used to manipulate and control others, supposedly in the name of love, are shame (*"I love you even though you are bad"*) and fear (*"I love you if you do what I say and don't make me punish you"*). Shame-induced love is not love at all, but a condescension and belittling of another while at the same time elevating oneself; fear-based love is not love at all, but a bullying and threatening of another — communicating *Love me, or suffer.*

Yeshua constantly called out the leaders of his time who presented themselves as perfect, revealing to the people that even the *perfect* leaders were no different than anyone else. But he did not do this via soapbox sermons and rants on the market corner speaking directly against them. He did so by blatantly loving the people the leaders blatantly condemned. Yeshua did not have to speak out against the leaders — the leaders spoke against themselves by vocally trying to create and maintain the separation between *us* and *them*, while Yeshua's actions instead closed the gap of *us* and *them*. The way Yeshua disregarded their attempted shaming of himself and instead chose the most loving action in each situation put the leaders to shame instead. All the people saw and discerned in their hearts that Yeshua's way — which is what his followers called their practice before it began to be called Christianity: *The Way* — was the most natural, best-feeling, and most connective way. The leaders realized this as well, saw the people responding, and recognized it as their greatest fear of losing power coming true.

The way our own societies and religious organizations have once again become places of shaming and blaming, both directly and indirectly, is just as harmful as the leaders of Yeshua's time. People are told right out they are not good enough and need to ask forgiveness for being human, for being who they are. When love is spoken of, it is often in the same condescending, unworthy tones that imply they now owe the one who is loving them, whether that one is God or the person saying *I love you* to them. The implication is that they are now indebted to do what they are told is *good* and *right*, or they're out in the cold once again.

This is love with strings attached.

Is it possible to completely disregard all blame and shame

and debt and need for forgiveness and instead just love?

Why do we think we must be saturated in feelings of guilt and unworthiness in order to understand the contrast of a powerful, unconditional love?

Can't we simply love and be loved?

When people are manipulated and inspired toward love as a means of making amends or buying their way back from punishment from *bad* things, it becomes nothing more than trying to live by actions, to earn a love that is given freely in the first place. They are threatened with the image of an angry God always watching to catch, convict, and condemn, even though that does not match with the example Yeshua gave. When the leaders condemned and cast out a member of the community, Yeshua went to the house of that outcast for dinner. He knew we are fully God in this place, and he knew God — *love* — does not behave that way.

In our times and rituals, would Yeshua deny people who wish to participate in the eucharist, the communion of the Lord's Supper symbolism of the bread and wine expressing commitment to his Way simply because they weren't yet an official member of his group? Would Yeshua turn away people who want to help serve and love others alongside him merely because they have lived life in all its mess and possibly experienced divorce, despair, or any other frowned-upon experience prior to volunteering to serve? Would Yeshua reject a person and their inspired message, claiming it could not possibly have come from God because it did not come from the proper and expected source and method?

We are God, and the image we demonstrate to others is shaping their view of the world and, in turn, their image of God, of the universe they live in. The only angry and hateful God, then, is the God *we* portray and embody to others on the street, in the grocery store, in our living room. The only angry and hateful God *we* see is in the people around us, who are each in their own temporary moments of trying to find their way the best they can. But when those angry and hateful people happen to be members of our immediate family, such as a parent, it shapes our image and relationship with the energy of God tenfold.

Another face that has been given to God is that of a father. This is perhaps the most familiar description used in describing God to ourselves and others, and this image does fit well for many people. Realizing that God is love and that love made everything, including us, we realize we are products of love — the children of love. Love is our parent.

Yeshua himself encouraged his friends to visualize the energy of God this way, saying *When you pray, when you reach out to cross the distance and connect with the energy of God, do it like this: Our Father who is all around us, we quiet ourselves to recognize you are the energy and purity in all things. May all beings come to know you and be you. We trust that we will have all we need this day, as we remember that we have never been let down before. We forgive those who have offended us as we ask forgiveness of anyone we may have offended ourselves. Help us to find and choose the most loving way in every circumstance, and deliver us from all separation.*

It is important to understand and remember that any face or symbol is just that: a tool to assist our human minds in relating to its senses and its world around it. Visualizing the energy of God as a parent may be exactly how one person can tap into that energy best, but it may be a completely useless concept to another. There are many whose human parents were not so unconditionally loving, or were outright abusive, making it very difficult and even repulsive for them to think of God as a parent. For them, maybe visualizing the energy of God as the Universe all things are in, the atoms everything is made of, or any other concept and imagery they are comfortable with may be the connection they need. God *is all and is in all*, so there can be no wrong way to relate to this energy and the love that it is.

I learned far more what the energy of God is like when I became a parent myself than I did from years of studying books and experimenting with traditions and practices. Love undeniably requires action. Love requires actually *doing* something. Actions speak louder than words. Being something, becoming directly involved in something leads to a much greater understanding than simply observing from the sidelines or imagining what a thing is like, just as the best and quickest way to learn a new language is to live directly among the people whose language you want to learn—to dive right in.

When my daughter, Julia, was born, everything changed. Everything I'd ever imagined about being a parent or what it was like to love another being was shown to fall tremendously short of the real deal. I also began to understand many things my own parents must have felt, emotions and processes they must have gone through, and began to see why they may have done certain things, the human struggles they may have been experiencing and reacting from.

The greatest impact that happened to me in becoming a parent was having all images and notions I had struggled with of a punitive, angry, and judgmental parent-God completely tossed out the window. The instant I became a father, I knew that if the energy of God was like a father, there was no way on earth there was any room for delighting in holding anger and grudges, finding pleasure in dishing out punishments, or any form of hateful disapproval whatsoever. When we so deeply and naturally love something that came from us—something that is a *part* of us—no thought of joyfully catching them being *wrong* in any way and getting to throw them into time-out or a fiery pit for all eternity has any space to exist. In fact, we will overlook a million things and go out of our way to get them whatever they want, gladly going without something for ourselves to arrange things for them.

When our children are tiny and learning to walk, we don't scowl at them in disappointment or yell at them in anger when they only make it a step or two before falling. We spread our arms wide and smile and cheer and call encouragements out to them: *Come on, Baby! You can do it! You've got this! Look at you — you're doing it!* If we who are humans on earth can love our own children so unwaveringly even as they fail and fall, how can we imagine the energy of God being any different than this?

Many people who are not comfortable with or don't connect with certain images and faces they've had demonstrated to them often have difficulty with The Way. They have not been shown that the core of The Way is simply to love. They have been exposed to the polluted, manipulative version of The Way instead of the loving way, like the outcasts cut from the community in judgment and discrimination during Yeshua's lifetime. Like the people of different race or color or sexual orientation cut from our fellowship in our lifetime. *Us* versus *them* is not The Way.

But the same way our minds need to use symbols and imagery to process and connect to our world around us is the same way our minds also latch on to these images and often have such a hard time letting go of its concepts and experiences. Once we've been shown one version, it's hard to adopt a different version. Familiarity, and the comfortable place it brings, can also make it difficult for something new to grow.

I love and am moved by music, and like anyone I have certain favorite artists and musicians. Sometimes when one of my favorite bands or singers comes out with a new album, I get so excited about it, purchase it, sit down to listen to it straight through, and feel deeply disappointed. *I like the old album better. This sounds different than before. This is nowhere near as good as their last album.* all run through my mind. Yet in nearly every case, if I give it a few more listens, it begins to grow on me. I begin to learn the new material, and begin to realize that it actually *is* just as good if not better than their last album after all! I often end up loving the new work even more than I loved the older work, and I have reached the understanding that it is my mind and its familiarity comparing it to what existed before that says *Whoa, wait a minute – what is* this *crap?!* And in reality, who wants more of the exact same as before? Isn't it the new, the fresh, the brave, bold, new life we crave anyway?

Redefining concepts and rewiring the mind can be nearly impossible for some, and scary for everybody. It is extremely important that we be present, that we be love, that we be God for each other as we go through these processes. We need to remember that no matter how it's imagined or presented, it's only faces that have been painted on a canvas, for the purpose of communication and connection. It's not only perfectly okay to shred that canvas and paint a newer, more beautiful image that encompasses all we've personally experienced the energy of God to be, but we are *invited* to do so. The energy of God is a living, moving, breathing awareness that we live, move, and breathe in; it is a relationship that takes two. It is a two-way street.

It takes the entire community exemplifying a new way, a new life, to repair the levels of damage that have been done — a unity and commitment to work toward the healing of each individual, which will in turn spiral out toward the healing of the society as a whole.

It's not about being perfect at all.

It's simply about loving.

It's something that takes time, patience, and... love.

Love so God will think
"Ahhhhhhh,
I got kin in that body!
I should start inviting that Soul over
for coffee and rolls..."[8]

VOICE

UNDESERVED KINDNESS

MY CATS LOVE TREATS. My cats love kitty treats so much that once they are given a handful of treats to munch on, they wait approximately five minutes, then come ask for treats again, hoping the stupid humans have forgotten they just gave them treats.

Sometimes I hide treats around the house for them to find — happy little surprises for them to happen upon during their hunting expeditions, when they are pretending to be wild outdoor panthers as they examine and reexamine the same nooks and crannies of the house they've examined a thousand times before.

I leave random surprises for them because I love them, and I love to see them having fun and excited and happy and healthy. This is one way I can show my love and they can know they are loved and in a safe, loving place.

One of my favorite things to do for my children is surprise them with special treats like mysterious outings where I refuse to tell them where we are going until we pull into the parking lot and they're like *Wow, are we really going here?* It brings great joy to my heart to see them happy, and I love doing things for them for no reason at all, especially as the Aries in me gets too excited and impatient to wait for Christmas and birthdays to roll around. I believe actions like these are the best and most impacting way for them to know they are loved.

And I don't *have* to do these things; food in their bellies and a roof over their head is really all I'm required to do. I could just tell them I love them over and over, but the actions and energies always speak louder than words, and gestures that go above and beyond the minimum requirements are what drive the message home to their growing hearts and minds.

If I want to produce humans who love, I first have to love and be love.

If I want to send humans who know God and *are* God out into the world, they must understand that the energy of God is the energy of love in all things — and no amount of simply telling someone will drive that message home. Only the realization of seeing it in front of them and demonstrated to them, as well as the consistency of seeing it demonstrated to things and others who are *not* them will impart these messages unshakably to their hearts. As they observe me and my reactions to our environment, it is my responsibility to show them how to be love in this world.

These are mirrored reflections of the way the energy of God is speaking to us twenty-four seven — not in words and voices, but in actions and energies that communicate personalized messages to our growing hearts and minds. My children watch and listen and learn from me the same way we watch and listen and learn from the love that is the energy of God around us.

But how do *we* watch and listen and learn from the energy of God? How do we *know* the energy of God is love, other than simply being told it is? In this kind of world, how can we know — much less see — for ourselves that the underlying energy of everything is love?

In order to demonstrate and embody a thing, we must know it, believe it, and be it ourselves, but while living in a world so unbalanced and unjust, surrounded by pressures and hatred on every side, it is so very easy to allow even our own selves to slip away more each day, completely forgetting exactly who we are, and forgetting that there is good in this world. Bombarded with energies that create division and separation, we can quickly become lost and forget *we* are light and love and God on this planet. When this begins to happen, even the most passionate thing we stand for, that thing that ignites the fire in our bones and stirs our heart to action, can begin to fade as we clash and struggle with the world around us.

It's tremendously easy to drown this way.

My current day job is extremely demanding, with pressure and expectations to meet quotas, produce high accuracy, and miraculously multi-task answering phones, assisting walk-in members, and helping other co-workers, with all of it constantly rated and graded to judge my performance. Though none of these tasks are even what life is about to me, and none of it is what I'm alive in this body for, when any one of these demands are not met — and something is inevitably not met — I am still easily thrown into the whirlwind of *But can't you see I am literally exhausted and completely worn out from trying so hard to accomplish all these things, and it's still not good enough?* My mind can quickly slip into *Why do I even try anymore?*

When we are overwhelmed by the separating energies around us, and all we hear about is what we're not doing well enough or right enough, the discouragement that sets in can drag us to the bottom of a deep pit where nothing matters and we've forgotten who we are. When we stop caring, we then begin having urges toward thoughts, words, and actions that are even more destructive to ourselves and others, creating a repeating cycle of deeper and deeper separation. This makes us want to zone out and find a television or a drink or a drug or some other form of influence that matches the energy of and feeds the way we're feeling in the moment—though it is only for a moment. Yet even if we *are* consciously and mentally aware that these feelings are only temporary, only for a moment, it is still extremely easy for these human minds we have to give in and drown.

Life and all its highs and lows and messy, undesired circumstances are endless, and in those moments of discouragement, so far from the energy of love, it's difficult or even impossible to imagine finding the underlying love in a situation, or of *being* love ourselves again. We can't fathom ever being around the vibration of love again, and feel that the energy of love will ever be able to find us again, much less touch us or communicate with us.

We are separated.

We feel hopeless.

Then, as we load up to drive to the next thing demanding something from us, a song will begin playing on the radio the instant we start up our car and say *I see you've been fighting so long, and it's okay, no matter what you've done right, no matter what you've done wrong...* and then the very next song sings about how in the feelings of being crushed, in the feelings of being pressed, something new is being shaped… and the next song reminds us that we are still who we are, no matter what has happened, that nothing outside ourselves can ever change that… and it begins to dawn on us that we have heard from the energy of God — love *has* found a way to find us, love has not failed to reach out and touch us, love has communicated the most perfect message we needed to hear, at the most perfect time, in the most perfect and natural way, making use of whatever source is around us in the normal course of our daily life. We did not even have to do anything special; we did not have to go anywhere special. We only had to keep living, keep going.

And another layer is woven into our realization that at the bottom, in the back, behind anything that ever happens to us or around us, there is love, a foundation of goodness that is ultimately guiding us forward and onward — the energy of God that is able to work with anything and everything that happens and make it usable for good. The energy of God reshapes things to be the best thing that thing can be for all those it affects.

Everything is love, so everything can *be* love for you.

Everything is God, so everything can be God for you.

There is nothing different or special that needs to be done in order to receive the messages we need from love, no specific ritual or ceremony required to find the love that is still present — and it is always present, in every circumstance, no matter how dark the world may seem around us.

Yet there is still a part of us, embedded from the society and world we are members of, that can't help but whisper *But I did this and this and this, and I reacted this way and that way, and I completely crashed here and here and here, and my actions, my words, my thoughts were so far from loving — why would I still even be allowed to come close to any form of love? Why would any shape of love want anything to do with me? I do not deserve this.*

But this is how love is.

This is *what* love is.

Love is undeserved kindness.

And love is undeserved kindness, *even toward yourself.*

As the end of Yeshua's final week drew near, he began to intensify his attempts to help the people understand that undeserved kindness was exactly what his message was. His only aim was to teach everyone — regardless of status — that love does not care if someone has successfully earned or miserably failed to deserve being loved as that world told them, and as our world continues to tell us is the way things are. Rewards and punishments, acceptance and rejection, compliance and rebellion all have no lines in love. The energy of God knows no borders such as these.

And he knew God could be heard in any way, from any source, at any time.

When I am no longer among you, he told them, *do not be afraid. Do not worry who will lead you or how you will be able to find your way — the same spirit that guides me is the same spirit that guides you. We are all one. You are no different from me. The spirit of God is within you; the kingdom has been here all along. Once you learn to turn within and hear the Voice, it will be as if you've stumbled upon a boundless treasure that has been in your own home all along, and you will be able to do even greater things than I have done.*

Yeshua knew and could see that no matter how many times he illustrated and demonstrated the concepts of The Way to them, the programming and conditioning of their minds still activated and overrode their responses and reactions — and would continue to do so for quite a long time. He knew he would not always be with them, and they would need to know how to see to the center of the truth themselves. He understood and had to be okay with the fact that all he could do was plant the seeds, sow the acorn ideas that would gradually begin to grow from generation to generation toward becoming the mighty oak tree that will one day reach into heaven, that energy where suffering has been eliminated.

We are each a leaf of that tree; we have the power to reach into the kingdom, and when we do, every other leaf and branch and root will feel it and see it and know it on some level.

This spirit that is inside every one of us is how we are able to find the most loving way, even in a world where bad things seem to happen to good people and good things seem to happen to bad people. This spirit is what we are made of; we can never be separated from it even if we want to be.

The separation and division we seem to feel in certain moments is an illusion—it is only one-sided, in our own minds. The energy of God never leaves us, can never leave us, and is always able to be tapped into and connected to, even by those who cause harm.

No matter what we go through, no matter what happens to us or around us, when we pause and turn our feelings and attention within us, we find the never-moving, ever-present, stillness of love. We return to love because it is what we are at our core. This is the still, small voice inside, the quiet intuition we can consult when attempting to come to a decision on any sort of matter, whether it is specifically called the energy of God or not.

This is how we tell the difference between right and wrong: we *feel* it. We know it from our connection to love like a radar system sending out radio waves. The actions and choices that bring us closer to love and brings love to a situation ping back to us the feeling of *the right way,* and the actions and choices that separate us farther from love and destroys love in a situation ping back to us the feeling of *the wrong way.*

Our world around us pressures us to think and act as they do: discriminate, judge, hate, exclude, reject, fight for our own recognition no matter the cost, and fear anyone and anything different than ourselves. It's in these moments it is so important for us to stop—even for a heartbeat—and think for ourselves, asking *Am I really okay with this? Is this really how I want to be? Is this what I choose to put out into this world?*

Anyone who claims to be in the light, but still hates another, is still in the darkness.

Those of us who are driven by the light and the love continue on, no matter what happens. We may fall for a moment, we may need to sit and heal for a minute, but we always rise, we always come back to shine again.

It is our DNA.

It is how we are the image of God.

It is how we are God.

So we are driven to continue stretching our hand out into the darkness, groping for love, reaching for light, and when we feel love grip our hand in return, we also feel the strength and bravery required to act on that love, the power to become a channel of light in this world. Sometimes we are the giver of the energy of God, and sometimes we are the receiver of the energy of God. We are always able to find the way to be love and to receive love in the best way possible, for whatever the situation. Sometimes that's something as little as gifting a smile to a passing stranger or simply being a silent presence listening to another person venting or ranting in an attempt to express their feelings and emotions into words outside their flailing mind.

The more we grow aware of the way the energy of God communicates through everything around us in our daily lives, the easier it becomes to hear and receive those messages, and a feeling that we are never alone begins to permeate every fiber of our being. We then also begin growing more and more open and able to be a natural channel of love and light: a messenger of God for others in this place—all without ever having to do anything extra beyond our normal, routine daily lives.

Suppose a brother or a sister
is without clothes and daily food.

If one of you says to them,
"Go in peace;
keep warm and well fed,"

but does nothing about their physical needs,

what good will it do?

Claiming to love others,
but never showing so in actions,

is hypocrisy.[9]

HOME

I AM NOT OKAY

AS IT CONTINUED TO become clear to Yeshua that continuing to deliver his message would most definitely lead to the ending of his time here, and that there truly was no other way, he could have easily drifted into the darkness of resentment toward the people's ignorance and stubbornness. He could have lost all patience with the way they simply could not understand his message no matter how hard he worked, no matter how many different methods he used to try to communicate it to them. He could have grown furious in anger at them, knowing that even though he did everything he did for them in pure love, they would still end up in the place where they would rather kill him than put forth effort toward change on their own parts.

Yet, miraculously, he didn't.

Instead, his love and compassion for the people only increased and never wavered, even though his own mind was in turmoil and wrestled with the inevitability of his fate.

As the end grew near, he began to shift his strategy, and started to more openly prepare his closest friends as well as the crowds for his death. *The light is among you for only a little while longer. Take action, aim for changes while you have the light, or the darkness you are about to experience ahead might overwhelm you. The light shines on the good and the evil without discrimination. While you still have the light, do as the light does, love as the light loves, so that you may become children of light.*

The people he was even more concerned about were those who *did* accept his messages and *had* begun to do their best to shift into being love in this place. He knew how much they still depended on him and relied on him to teach them and show them the loving way. He knew that when the time came for him to leave, these crowds could so easily fall into confusion, disappointment, and depression—a darkness that could seem even worse than the oppression they had been used to and had been living in to begin with. The new awareness of another way they now knew would never allow them to go backward and still be okay. They needed to understand that it was not specifically himself they needed, but their own connection to the same greater energy he operated from.

We're no different than this in our own time. It is incredibly easy for our minds to become attached to our teachers, our gurus, and our pastors, clinging to the desire for them to be always available to us, and always perfect. When any one of them leave, die, or make human mistakes, our dependency is exposed, and we can be thrown into a whirlwind. This is why it is said that the best teachers only point the way, and make the student do the actual walking. Then, when the teacher is no more, the student is able to confidently stand on their own because they did it all on their own to begin with.

Our human tendency is to look outward. Something in us is naturally aware that we are in some sort of *in*-ness, and that we are somehow looking *out*. This sense arises from the way we came from spirit, are spirit, and are returning to spirit, but our physical minds here with their visualizations of separation interpret these feelings to mean that there will also be an outer person or thing coming to take us out of this inner — something or someone *other* that will come rescue us, save us. Like the people in Yeshua's day, we, too, have misunderstood these feelings, and been waiting for an external savior. We look for the next gifted leader to take us into a better future, the next fantastic invention and technology to solve all our problems, the arrival of extraterrestrial beings or some other form of savior to come hit a reset button and wipe out all the bad and the difficult so only the good and the easy will remain forevermore. Yet all along, it has always been *our* decision, *our* responsibility to choose which direction we are going to go. Change begins with us — inside us — and spirals *out* from us.

This is the way it has always been, and this is the way it remains for us today.

Yeshua experienced this same humanness, crying *My soul is beyond troubled, but what shall I say: 'Father save me from this hour'? No, it is for this very purpose I have come to this hour...*

The message Yeshua needed his followers and everyone who came after them — which includes us — to understand was that they were not alone, had never been alone, and would never be alone. The connection to the Way of Love each one of them carried within themselves was strong enough and unshakable enough to depend on, and could be trusted to guide them the same way he had been guiding them during his brief time physically present with them.

Whoever believes in the way I have taught them is not believing in me, but in the way I've come from, and the way they themselves have come from. Whoever sees the things I do sees the natural way we are meant to be. It is not my light, but their own inner light they recognize calling them out of the darkness. Yet if anyone hears these words and sees these ways, but does not keep them, I do not judge them in any way — I did not come to judge the world but to light the world. Each one, by their own choices and actions, judge themselves plenty enough without anyone else adding to it. Instead, our only responsibility is to love them.

The more we are connected to the wholeness of the Way and doing our best to live every aspect of our lives from the most loving space possible, the easier and easier we will find it to choose the most loving way in each situation. We will find it easier and easier to be able to give love to everyone and everything, no matter how difficult or negative or *bad* they may be — and as a bonus, we will also find it easier and easier to *receive* love. We find ourselves swimming in an ocean of love that knows no limits, and begin to realize that every person and every thing and every event that happens can be and is love in one form or another — the energy of God, ever-present with us.

But it always goes both ways. We can receive this boundless love and bathe in it and soak in it and absorb it and get high on *Oh isn't this wonderful? I am loved beyond anything I could ever do, no matter what I've ever done! I'm loved, I'm loved, I'm loved!* but then what? Is that where it stops? What do we do with this? Do we sit on it and just keep it for ourselves? Where do we go from here?

After this, we then have the responsibility to carry it out into the world, to pass it on to those around us.

And how could it be otherwise? Could any one of us truly accept boundless amounts of true, unconditional love in one moment and then turn around and do something hateful and harmful to another in the next moment?

If love has really permeated our system, it changes us.

It becomes us.

We become that.

We become love.

Yeshua illustrated this truth to the crowds one day by telling a story of a man who owed the ruler ten thousand credits. When the ruler had this man brought in front of his court to pay up and settle his debts, the man was unable to pay, so the ruler ordered that the man and all his family be thrown into prison. The man fell to the ground and begged for more time, pleading that he was working as hard as he could, wailing *Please! Be patient with me!* His pleading so moved the ruler's heart that he agreed to the man's request for more time and took it a step further — he dismissed the man's debt entirely! The man went dancing out of the palace, hardly able to believe his good fortune. But on his way back home, he came across his neighbor, who happened to owe the man one hundred credits. The man seized his neighbor and began choking him, demanding the one hundred credits he was owed. *Please! Be patient with me! I will get it paid back to you!* the neighbor pleaded, but the man refused and called the authorities to have the neighbor thrown into prison. Some of those who had been in the ruler's court earlier that day saw what the man did and reported it back to the ruler. The ruler then summoned the man once again. *Are you the man whose debt of ten thousand credits I just dismissed this morning?* The man answered *Yes, Sir, I am, and I am eternally grateful for your boundless generosity!* The ruler then stood up from his chair. *But*

I've just received word that you were seen aggressively demanding repayment from one in your community only moments ago? The man took a step backwards and swallowed. *Y-yes, Sir, but –* The ruler interrupted with a gesture and softly continued, *Considering the great kindness that was shown you this very morning, shouldn't you have been more willing to show the same toward your own neighbor?* At that, the ruler once again ordered the man be sent to prison, this time with torture to be administered, until his debt was repaid.

Selfishly, the man had not allowed the mercy that had been shown to him to reach his core, had not allowed it to so change his life that he *became* that same mercy. He did not pass the kindness and love forward, and ended up worse than he was before — suffering torture instead of merely being imprisoned.

This is not meant to say we owe the same in return to others or else we will regret it, but is saying that we often get what we give. What we put out is what will come back to us. What we put into our self, into our minds, and into our environment is what will come back out. This is what is called karma; this is the cause-and-effect of energy that is attracting and generating more of the same sort of energy.

Karma is often misunderstood as a form of punishment. Karma is not meant to be a blaming, not meant to be an accusation saying that all our problems and everything that happens to us is our own fault — if this is what it meant, it would be no different than the *good things will happen if you're good and bad things will happen if you're bad* oppression Yeshua spent his life speaking against. Things do happen as a result of our choices and actions in cause-and-effect chain reactions as karma describes, but it is not an inescapable force or some god-figure in the sky keeping score and doling out fines and punishments, and it is *not* meant to beat us down to a weak, resentful, and fearful frame of mind. We do not see karma at work in our lives because we are helpless against it, but because we have the power to rise above it. If a karmic situation is making us feel like we're suffering, it is in these sufferings and trials that we can find and remember the power we *do* have to direct the course of our life. Karma is not to punish, it is to uplift; it is a mirror reflecting back to us our own actions and gifting us the opportunity to say *Oh my, I don't think I like what I see — I need to make some changes*. When we remember how strong we are and take up the responsibility of taking charge of our lives and our choices, we are encouraged and uplifted — and since we are all connected, when we are uplifted, everyone is uplifted.

The torture Yeshua meant in the story of the ungrateful man was not a physical torture, but an internal, mental one. The man's ungraceful behavior had been brought to light in front of everyone, including himself, and the contrast he felt between the way of love and kindness and the actions he had chosen instead was torture to his soul. *Why, O why did I ever do that?!*

The karma he experienced from his choices and actions toward his neighbor showed him the importance of every thought and action, and how each directed and shaped his life.

When we are truly connected with the energy of God, we have an internal guidance system, directing us via our feelings to the most loving way possible.

And when we are truly connected with the energy of God, we don't *want* to keep it all to ourselves and sit on it — we want to go out and give to others, help others, serve others, love others, because that's what the energy of God is. That's what the energy of God does.

Why would we ever receive a love for ourselves, then just

keep it for ourselves, like possessing the only fire and leaving everyone else out in the cold and the dark? Can we be okay with essentially saying *Sorry for your luck, sucks to be you, better luck next time?* Even when we're experiencing the feelings of being in love with a physical romantic partner, we find ourselves in kinder, gentler, more generous and helpful moods toward everyone as we go through our day.

Whether we are consciously aware of it or not, our hearts and souls feel the differences and contrasts between the loving way and the unloving way, and it affects our health and mental states. When we learn to tune in to ourselves and follow the feelings leading us toward the natural way of love, we find ourselves never alone and guided in every life choice we face.

As our habits and lifestyles grow more loving and light-filled, we will begin to notice the contrast between ourselves and those who are not committed to love. We will begin to feel the difference in energies between things like movies, books, and other entertainment, and naturally begin to become unable to tolerate the unloving, harmful material. Distances will begin to grow even between friends and family because two opposing energies are unable to exist in the same place for long periods of time.

Yeshua taught about this difference in energy using the symbol of a shepherd — an image he used often because it was an extremely common thing every level of society was familiar with in that time and region. *The time will come when every soul from every nation will return to the source they came from, and the Father of us all will have to sort each one the way a shepherd sorts each animal from being with the herd in the field into their individual gates for their sleep: the sheep in their gate, the goats in theirs. Now, there are souls who live in love, and there are souls who do not. To those who love, he will say 'Come, you who blessed! Take your inheritance, for you renewed the kingdom of heaven on earth as it was in the beginning. When I was hungry, you fed me. And when I was thirsty, you gave me something to drink. I was alone as a refugee and you welcomed me into your homes and into your lives. I was naked and you gave me clothes to wear; I was sick and you tended to my needs. I was in prison and you did not forget about me.' And they will say 'Wow, really? When did we find you hungry and give you food? When did we find you thirsty and satisfy your thirst? When were you a foreigner and we welcomed you in, or find you naked and clothe you? When did we find you sick and nurse you to health? When did we visit you in prison?' And Love will reply, 'Whenever you did even the least of these kindnesses to a brother or sister you saw hungry or cold, you did it to me.'*

Then he will say to those who walked in ways apart from love, 'I am so very sorry, I really wanted you to be able to come into this gate with us. But I was hungry and you gave me nothing to eat, I was thirsty and you gave me nothing to drink. I was alone and you did not invite me in, I needed clothes and you left me naked, I was sick and in prison and you left me behind.' And they will say, 'Wait — what? When did we see you hungry or thirsty or in need of clothes or sick or in prison and did nothing to help you?' And Love will reply, 'Whenever you refused to do even the least of these kindnesses to a brother or sister, you refused to do it for me. I'm sorry, I don't know you.'

This illustration is unfortunately one of the most misused by those in leadership positions, taking it as their proof that there will be punishment and rejection when we die if we fail to do everything they say or if we don't live up to every rule and law they believe should be followed. It's even taken so far as to literally label people as sheep and goats, with goats being the bad people – more license to judge and discriminate others!

This takes the message out of context and completely misses Yeshua's point.

Yeshua was using examples from local daily life that those listening could relate to, and his aim was not to put fear and dread into them that they better measure up or else they're out of the club, it was to demonstrate that loving and serving and blessing each other is The Way.

We are not to size up our brothers and sisters to judge if they are sheep or goats, then go ahead and shut those deemed goats out of the gate here and now. We are to follow the example of Yeshua and invite them in to join us at our table, show them love that has not been earned, meet their needs regardless of whether they deserve it or not – or better yet, go out to where they are and ask them what they need most, ask them how we may best be of help to them.

Won't this have an even greater effect toward infecting them with love than essentially saying *If you'd only love, then you can come in – until then, stay out!*?

For a period of about fifteen years, I distanced myself from everything I had been raised in: the church, the faith, the people. During that time, I threw out everything such as these I had been taught and told. I explored everything I wanted to and studied anything I was curious about, without fear or concern of taboos or punishments. When my journey led me full circle back to the place I'd started from, I found I had new eyes and a new mind. I left everything from my first experiences out the window and sought the sources of it all for myself. I kept all my previous misgivings and resentments and traumas silenced in the background as I allowed the foundations to reveal the truth of things to me on their own. What rebuilt from researching for myself took a completely different shape than I had had projected to me all my life.

What I found at the base of everything, and was surprised to find, both old and new, was love — love that had been twisted into various unnatural forms in different areas. Anything can be twisted and manipulated to accommodate the purposes and aims of the one twisting it, and this love that is at the foundation of life is no exception. In many places, it has become unrecognizable as love at all. I discovered that the summarized *Sunday versions* of things did not always include the whole story, and at times even ignored the surrounding context the story came from, completely changing its message and meaning. I was repeatedly surprised to find unknown details and differences in popular and well-known stories and references.

For example, one verse my father quoted to my siblings and I all during our childhood, telling us he believed it was the life purpose statement for our family, was *You shall be called the repairer of the breach.* By itself, this could really be anything one wishes to paint it as, from an image of a grand savior to a road construction worker. A pressure and expectation to live up to this was impressed onto us, without any context of what it would entail, how to become this, or even what it truly meant.

Then, when I returned to this passage and read the chapter it had been extracted from in its entirety, I found that single verse was actually only the tail end of a message from God to the people via the prophet Isaiah: *Shout out loud! Do not be silent! Hold nothing back — tell the people exactly where they've gone off track! Say to them 'You come to the temple every day and seem delighted to learn all about my ways. To all who look from the outside, it appears you are a nation of right-living people, law-abiding and full of the energy of God. Yet you are performing your rituals for your own selves; when you humble yourselves, it is for the pats on the back you receive from your brothers and sisters – and all the while you keep oppressing those below you! What good are these things when you keep on fighting and quarreling? You render all your efforts meaningless with this inauthentic behavior! You make a show of going through all the motions, bowing your heads like reeds bending in the wind, putting on pious, sad faces and parading around dressed in rags, covered in ashes. Do you think those are the sort of things I want? Do you think that is the sort of energy I am? No. This is the sort of behavior I want to see: To break the chains of injustice, to lighten the burdens of those around you, to free the oppressed, to forgive debts and offenses, to share your food with the hungry, to give shelter to the homeless, to meet the needs of those among you, and to be present and available to your own families. Stop pointing your finger and spreading vicious rumors! Stop shifting blame and avoiding responsibility! Do these, and your light will shine out from the darkness that surrounds you; the darkness around you will be as bright as noon. You will always have the sense of where to go and what to do next. You will have a full life in the emptiest of places and be like a well-watered garden, an ever-flowing spring that will never run dry. You will be able to use the rubble of the past to build anew, to rebuild the strong foundations. You will be known as those who can repair the breaches caused by separation, heal old wounds, and restore the health of the community once again.'*

The entire message and basis of becoming and being known as healers of the community, repairers of gaps and separations is to love, to serve, and to be there for each other, meeting each other's needs. This should not be a thing people are surprised to find the deeper they look – it should be something people *expect* to find!

We *can't* stop at receiving love only for ourselves. We must act fairly, love mercy, walk humbly. We must clothe ourselves with compassion, kindness, gentleness, humility, and patience.

Another excessively-quoted verse I discovered had more to its context is actually foretelling Yeshua's arrival and the energy of God he would demonstrate and embody. The single verse is popular as simply *Those who hope in the Lord will renew their strength; they will soar with wings like eagles – they will run and not grow weary, they will walk and not faint.* But again, backing up to read the entire chapter, we find *Speak comforting words to those who feel they are waiting in darkness: A branch will emerge to bear fruit – a child! And on this child, the Spirit of the Eternal One will alight and rest. By the Spirit of wisdom and discernment, he will shine like the dew. By the Spirit of counsel and strength, he will interact fairly and act courageously. By the Spirit of knowledge and reverence of the Eternal One, he will take pleasure in honoring the natural, Eternal ways. He will demonstrate the way of fairness and equity; he will consider more than he sees with his eyes, and listen to more than he hears with his ears, so that even those who can't afford a good defense will nevertheless get a fair and equitable chance. With just a word, he will end wickedness and abolish oppression. With nothing more than the breath of his mouth, he will destroy evil. He will clothe himself with authenticity and truth, and the impulse to right wrongs will be in his blood. The Way he will be an example of will give strength to the weary, and increase power to the weak. They will soar on wings like eagles; they will run and not grow weary, they will walk and not be tired.*

At the base foundation of everything is justice, equality, and love.

How can we be okay with anything else?

I am not okay with hatefulness or harm to anyone or

anything, not because of any bad karma it may accumulate or any fear of punishment or any negative image it may portray of myself to others, but because it is what *feels* best — what feels *right*.

It is what I know to be right, to my core.

In times I have been with the church and in times I have been apart from the church, my greatest desire and the cry of my heart has always been to know the heart of God, in whatever form or language that concept can be shaped into. In every environment I found myself in, my ever-present goal was to find and embody the heart of God. I needed to, and still need to, discover and assimilate that energy wherever it is found.

This didn't always mean being surrounded by people and things that embody this energy. Sometimes the energy of God was found in being surrounded by what the energy of God is *not*. When we are able to set aside our fears and judgments, we find we are equally able to learn about a thing both by being around that thing and by *not* being around it. The contrast of being confronted with what we are not seeking lights the way to what we *are* seeking.

It has always been in loving, serving, blessing others, and offering others space for healing themselves that I have found God — and every path, every religion, every philosophy has their own forms of these.

Yet even though instructions and teachings on these things are found in every place, in every journey, it is not always easy to do them. We can come up against resistance, ridicule, and rejection. Our minds want to have things be easy and pleasant, to accomplish things without requiring much effort, and to run away to where it doesn't feel like a constant battle to keep our fire burning in the middle of such a negative and threatening world.

In this world, in this physical existence, there will always be trouble, there will always be something you'd rather be another way than it is, but take heart: I have shown you how you can overcome this world, Yeshua taught. *Don't work so hard at trying get out of this world or to be separate from this world — remember you are the light in this world — but work at transforming and strengthening your mind so you may keep yourselves from harm and separation, which is the only evil in this world.*

Yeshua knew what it felt like to be misunderstood and resisted at every level. At times he felt like an alien himself, a refugee in his own homeland. He could have allowed himself to become frustrated with this place and just wanted to leave regardless of whether his work was done or not. But it was his vision for the way things could be, the way things were supposed to be, and the mismatch of the way it actually was around him that drove him on.

I identify with this aspect of the human Yeshua as well. For most of my life, I've felt as if I'm from another place. I've struggled with the overwhelming feelings that the things I see around me are not how things were supposed to be. I longed to separate from city life, from the crazy life of the western world here. As I connected more and more to our earth and these natural rhythms of living and interacting, I even began to hate cement, because it blocked the earth, covering so much of its surface from being touched directly. I was desperate for community and unity and an open-minded coexistence that delighted in differences instead of hating and killing them. And I couldn't see how the tiny droplet I was could possibly make any sort of difference in this ocean — it was too far gone, wasn't it?

It was so easy to sink into discouragement and focus only on getting to *that other place*, giving up everyone and everything here as lost and a waste of time. Community was never going to be possible, and there was never going to be any sort of environment that would be conducive to and supportive of practicing the values of this inner foundation that refused to let me go.

But then I gradually began to realize I was already doing these things within me, no matter where I found myself — *despite* wherever I found myself. I began to understand I was already operating from this foundation even in the midst of the mundane busy-ness of daily life in the city. It was who I was; it was a part of me regardless of where I was or what was happening around me. I *couldn't* be any other way, and nothing was truly stopping me or changing me, even when it felt like it was most of the time. A major key to my discovery of this was the realization that I *could* still feel the earth even through the cement. It dawned on me that it was because the cement *is still* the earth, still the same stuff as the earth, still the same energy I am and you are. The only blocking and separation was in my mind.

My journey has taken me from complaining about how this or that could be better or how those things over there should be another way, and from wanting to leave to find somewhere else that had these things the way I felt they should be, to realizing that maybe I was here for a reason. I was born where I was for a reason. I was born into the place and the community I'm in for a purpose. From outside of the whole, I can't make any difference. From inside the whole, I can make all the difference.

I am a part of the whole. The whole is not whole without me. And that means *you* are a part of the whole as well. The whole is not whole without you. How can I see you any other way? To label you and treat you any other way is to ask for separation and suffering—suffering for myself as much as for you.

Perhaps instead of moaning about being different and being strangers in a strange land and not having a community, we should instead delight that we are at least one light present, and begin redesigning our home here to match these visions.

We have visions for our families, for our churches, for our cities, for our planet.

We can no longer justify the desire to leave and find other places that already hold these visions while the places we are currently at lacks them. We have to begin taking part and begin *being* these things, begin being the energy of God in the world—being the Kingdom.

Even when he was feeling frustrated and discouraged, Yeshua didn't give up and abandon this world, because he knew this was home. He knew it was written that the energy of God made this place, looked at it, and called it good—it did not shrug and say, *Eh, this'll do for now.*

Can we be as we are, where we are, without shunning it and trying to get somewhere else?

We are lights here.

This is our home.

When I was younger,
and first learning I could feel
the presence of the Earth,
I would get SO annoyed
and upset with concrete
blocking the way and covering up
so much of the ground
everywhere I went.
I became anti-cement
nearly to an extreme
anti-civilization frame of mind,
until I grew a bit more
and found
cement did not matter,
asphalt was no block to Mother
because it WAS the Mother,
made of the same.
Then
after I had grown even more,
I figured out
that sameness was also me —
and that sameness was
only energy.

I can look at the tree
and see its sprig of a sprout
and its vulnerable twig
it grew from
as well as the towering
being it has become,
and feel overcome
with feelings
of honoring pride and joy
as if it were myself
who accomplished that,
because it was.

I look at my daughter,
who used to be so tiny
and helpless
and dependent on me,
now five years old
attending school
and needing her daddy
much less than before,
and even amid that awareness of change
I am overwhelmed
with pride and love
at the young lady she is becoming
all on her own,
this being so amazing
and completely herself,
and I watch and I know
this too is how
my own journey was.

I feel so old,
so wonderfully old…
I've been through so much,
learned levels on levels
of myriad things,
and still I know nothing,
nothing at all,
except Love is the one thing
that matters to me,
that binds every facet
of time across space,
and is the only true constant
growing each change.[10]

MIND

GOD BLESS YOU

YESHUA SELECTED A LARGE bowl and began filling it with water, softly humming one of the traditional festival tunes as he watched the water rise from the depths of the bowl. He smiled sadly to himself, the symbolism of daily life in front of him never escaping his notice — the voice of God speaking through all things.

The water reminded him of the time at the beginning of his mission he had stood in line with the rest of the people to be symbolically washed in the river — baptized — by his cousin, John. This had been one of his first public actions, starting his work with this open declaration that he was no different than anyone else. An echo of John the Baptizer's exclamation when seeing Yeshua drifted through his mind: *Look! There goes the lamb of God!* The meaning of that spontaneous declaration was now all-too-clear.

In the rising water he also saw a vision of his hopes and intentions. Having a sense of what was about to happen over the next few days, Yeshua mentally reviewed his beliefs and his knowledge of the truth. He knew that though the energy of life may be poured out like this water, it is not the end — it will rise again, and again.

His closest friends were still sitting over at the table, puzzling out and discussing among themselves what the unusual way Yeshua had just led them in the traditional feast could possibly mean. It was the annual festival of Pesach, the remembering of the Pass-Over, and someone was supposed to tell the story of how the energy of God had inspired their reluctant ancestor named Moses to confront the Pharaoh of Egypt and free their people from the slavery and oppression they had been living in. Moses had petitioned the Pharaoh for months, and many mysterious plagues and hardships had happened as signs that Moses really was acting in guidance from the energy of God. The final convincing had been when the first-born son of every household, including the Pharaoh's heavily-guarded palace, had died suddenly in a single night, except for those who had marked their houses to openly state they acknowledged the energy of God. Death had *passed over* these marked houses. After this event, the people were finally allowed to leave Egypt to find their own land, and Egypt had been left to do for themselves all the work the slaves had been doing. The people had then lived nomadically in the desert forty years until they finally crossed the river to their new permanent home, the same home Yeshua and his friends still lived in.

It had always been a past-tense story, but tonight Yeshua had told it in present-tense, as if it were happening right now, and his friends were trying to figure out why he had done it this way. They thought of the way Yeshua always called himself the *Son of Man*, while the crowds had taken the habit of calling him the first-born *Son of God*—was he telling them that he was a son about to die, as it had happened back in Egypt so long ago? The crowds had also been speculating that Yeshua was Moses reincarnated—was he trying to tell them this was actually true? What everyone wanted most was for Yeshua to take up his power and become their new ruler, to free them from their current oppression—was he telling them that, like Moses, he was finally about to lead them to freedom and begin his reign? The more scholarly of his followers had already recognized that Yeshua had literally retraced the path of Moses when he began his mission, first reenacting the time spent in the desert, then launching his teachings of love by coming into the same land by crossing the same river the people who left Egypt had finally crossed to reach this land of their own. Moses had never made it across the river, but maybe Yeshua had done this to show he was now completing the cycle that had not been finished before.

Then, after the story, he had continued beyond the traditional recounting of the history, taking a loaf of bread and holding it up for them all to see. *Our lives are no different than this bread – here for a moment, gone the next; whole now, later broken and consumed. Take it, eat it anyway, without fear. Life is eternally of the same energy; all things are of the same Father. We come from the Father, and we return to the Father. Live. Love. Lose. We are forever one with each other, and there is never any lack. Each time you partake of any of these, you honor all life, and you remember me.*

While they had still been pondering these words, Yeshua had oddly then seemed to switch to a traditional wedding ceremony, picking up his goblet of wine and holding it up the same. *All of you whom I have loved, and shown how to love, and shown how to be love, this is my proposal to you: if you accept this cup I offer, if you will endeavor to continue following all these things I have been for you, you will enter into promise and union with me and all I stand for. Like this wine, my energy – my life blood – will run through your bodies and through your lives, giving strength and guidance. Like this wine – my life blood – you will at times suffer for this union. But I will be with you, and each time you drink, you will remember me.*

Yet if you do not accept this cup, you are still never abandoned – the cup will eternally be poured out for you; drink, and find love.

And now he had removed his outer clothing and wrapped a large towel around his waist. He brought the bowl filled with water to his bewildered friends at the table and knelt in front of one. Removing his friend's sandals, he began to wash their feet—normally the job of a servant! The friend quickly pulled his foot away and cried, *No! What are you doing?! You shouldn't be washing my feet like a servant! You're my teacher – I should be washing your feet!* Yeshua looked up at his dear friend from the floor and smiled softly. *Don't you understand what I'm doing? You call me teacher, and you're right – I am. But you are also my teacher, and the student is not greater than the teacher. If I then, your teacher, have bared myself and sat in the dirt to serve you with this kindness, you should also be willing to do the same – whatever it takes to meet the needs of those you wish to love.*

Love everyone, as I have loved you.

This is how all people will recognize the energy of God.

Then Yeshua continued washing all their feet as a blessing to each, one by one, including the feet of the one he knew was about to betray him, including the one he knew would disown him, including the one he knew still doubted despite all he had witnessed firsthand. Regardless of who they had been or what they had done or what they would do in the future, Yeshua embraced and loved each one equally.

In our times as well as in Yeshua's, to offer a blessing to another is to show recognition of value in that other. A blessing is the highest honor that can be given, and for a blessing to even be possible, there can be no unforgiveness or anger in the same space. To even be capable of blessing another, there must be no animosity, no anger, no resentment present. There cannot be.

A blessing and *But I'm going to keep holding on to this grudge I have with you, I'm going to stay angry and bitter about things that have happened in the past, I'm not going to forgive you completely* simply cannot exist together. Like the inability of darkness to exist when there is a light switched on, a blessing is unable to be a blessing when there is not a sincere acceptance of the one being blessed and all that has happened before with them. Forgiveness of any and all perceived wrongs and offenses received from the one being blessed must be present, as well as a conscious choice to continue forward in an attitude of unconditional love toward that one — otherwise a blessing is just hollow words recited in an empty and dead ritual.

The very act of giving a blessing is giving approval, and there can be no approval with any form of hatred or judgment hovering between the two. There can be no approval without love, and to love is to bless — to *desire* to bless, to desire the very best for the other, purely and naturally, from the heart core.

To bless, to honor, to love: this is where God is.

Yeshua chose to love and serve everyone, no matter what they'd done or not done, or would do or would not do, whether they were close friends, total strangers, sick, healthy, rich, poor, young, old, educated, uneducated, male, female, nice, mean, foreigners, or enemies.

This was his intentional choice.

His mind was committed to love, no matter what.

Our minds control so much of our lives, from our physical bodies, thoughts, and attitudes, to the way we perceive and react to the world around us. Our minds are extremely impressionable and influenced by everything we are subjected to and surrounded by. The old saying that goes *You are what you eat* is especially true with our minds; the mental food we feed our minds is what we become. If we allow negativity, bitterness, resentment, violence, and hatred to saturate our minds, this world around us will appear to be a horrible, rotten, scary place with everyone and everything out to get us. If we embrace positivity, forgiveness, generosity, nonviolence, and love, making an effort to choose these whenever possible — and they are *always* possible — we are able to find and see the light shining from all the cracks and brokenness of this world. We are able to *be* the light shining into the cracks of this world. This world may still be a scary place, but in this way, we are able to remain hopeful and keep from sinking into dark pits of despair. Love gives us a solid grip that does not slip, even when violence and hatred is all around us.

Our minds can't tell a difference between reality and fantasy, between our waking life and our dreamtime. Part of our environment is the television shows we choose to watch, the movies we choose to attend, the video games we choose to play, the music we choose to listen to, and the people we choose to surround ourselves with. If we watch or read a lot of hateful and violent material, our mind doesn't know the difference between the real world and the fictional world — it only knows what is put before it to process and absorb. If we watch or read a lot of material that demonstrates kindness and growth-inspiring stories that remind us there *is* good in the world, and that there *are* good people in the world, then our minds reflect and assimilate these energies and begin to apply them toward what it then puts out: the way we act, and who we become. We see the possibility to become one of those good people in this world, one of these lights. The desire to become this begins to grow within us as a natural result.

Yet holding our focus on positive things cannot be allowed to become a denying of the realities and truths of this world. It can be so easy for our minds to wrap these traits around ourselves as a way to bury our heads in the sand and sweep the things we don't like and don't want to acknowledge under the rug of pretending it doesn't exist. This is as inauthentic as the hypocrites who pose so righteously and spiritually on the outside but lack sincerity and substance within.

Choosing to live in love is the path that feels best, but it is not the easiest path. Choosing to see the world as beautiful and full of love is not a free ticket to live our lives inside a bubble, disconnected from the realities around us. In fact, truly living in love will not *allow* us to sit idly by and wish others well from the comfort of our sacred spaces — it boils inside us and cannot remain silent or still at the sight of injustices and discriminations. Which of us would merely stand by smiling as our children are dragged away and treated unfairly, saying *It's all right, God will do something about it* instead of taking action ourselves? Not one of us.

If we do have past lives and reincarnate on this earth over and over, I have surely lived several lives as a monk or a nun, cloistered away inside a monastery somewhere. I have a strong introverting urge to stay in my own world with my familiar routines, quite content to be alone with my personal studies and writings and other artistic creativities. But if this was the case in other lives, something has snapped in this life. Something changed: the more I research, the more I look into things and feel into things for myself, the more and more I am unable to justify keeping to myself. I cannot come up with any excuses that hold water for not reaching out in love, not serving, not blessing, not healing, not speaking up for those abused and discriminated against. How can I ever rationalize denying to those in need what is in my capacity to gift? It is a responsibility I cannot ignore.

Yeshua chose to love others as if they were his own children, no matter what; his choice to love would not allow him to simply stand by, no matter what damage it would cause to his own reputation, no matter what damage it would cause between himself and his immediate family, no matter what damage it would cause to his own body.

Everyone we see treated unjustly, everyone we see in need, everyone we see suffering is our own child.

Compassion is a major tenet and focus of Buddhism. There is a deep, unshakable understanding that everyone and everything are all pieces of the same whole, forever connected, forever inseparable. What is done to another or even to one's own self affects and influences others, so a great responsibility to love, to give, and to serve is chosen as a way of life. One way followers of Buddhism visualize and generate love for others is to imagine each person, each animal, and each plant has been, and is, their mother, the one who gave birth to them and brought them into this world where they are able to experience this precious life; they respect and treat each person and each thing as if they themselves would not exist without this other.

It is a blessing to be able to experience life here—who would want to harm the one who gifted such a blessing?

Whenever we choose a thing, whether it's an action or a wish, our minds respond, and begin to search and scramble for ways to accomplish the mission we've given it. This is the fantastic way it's programmed, yet sometimes this programming doesn't know when to stop. It homes in on its goal with a death grip, and begins to stress out and panic if that goal is not attained quickly enough. It begins to feel unhappy and afraid it will never reach the goal. Its mission that originally aimed for happiness and love for ourselves and others becomes a wasteland of suffering. In this way, it creates hell instead of heaven—it creates suffering.

Yeshua knew that much of the suffering we experience is mental in nature. We so easily look outside ourselves, look at things just out of our reach that we don't have and wish we had, and long and pine for those things. We focus on the lack of what we don't have, driving ourselves crazy with the desire for what we don't have, causing suffering and misery for ourselves.

A balance between going for the goal and getting the goal must to be found and maintained.

Everything takes time, and comes into being in its own time. When we look back across our lives and see our own progress and path, we recognize where we were at different times in our lives and where we are today. We can realize we did not get here all at once, but only by a slow, step-by-step process. We grew up little by little, and this is no different than the growth process of our minds.

Yeshua could have simply organized communities or a kingdom and implemented a list of rules to follow and behaviors for people to act out in order to accomplish his vision.

That's certainly what the people around him wanted him to do; they didn't want to wait for the kingdom Yeshua taught them about to develop and grow—they wanted it now! They were accustomed to simply following rules and acting in the appropriate ways prescribed to them. Instead, Yeshua only focused on loving and serving, and on directing others how to love and serve. He planted these seeds everywhere he went so they would begin to take root and eventually grow shoots and branches that would connect with the branches others had grown within themselves over time. One day these branches would bridge all gaps and become the community and kingdom he knew was possible.

Everything in this world is about growing up.

A child expects and wants and needs, and is disappointed if something does not happen or takes too long to happen. They leave, running away to find something else to try to satisfy their wants.

An adult understands how things work, and stays and waits it out, waits to see what will develop from the seeds that have been planted, the events that have been set in motion. An adult understands they can prune and shape and tweak the growth *as it grows*. An adult has realized that if a thing is manifested instantly, already whole and complete, there will be no room to tweak anything that may need to be adjusted afterwards.

When I was a child, I talked like a child, I understood like a child, I thought like a child, but now that I've grown some, I begin to put away childish things.

We stay and wait.

It is so easy for our mind to feel at ease and all right when everything is going well and working properly, well-funded and peaceful; it's much more difficult for our mind to relax when things are not going well and falling apart, when money is running out or has run out and everything is tense with conflict and stress. When things are going how we want them to, we are in a great mood, we feel happy and joyful, we see the world with light hearts and find the positivity and humor in everyday things. When things are not going how we would like them to go or think they should go, our natural urge is to grip things tighter, trying to force them into submission, all the while dreading and worrying *What if it doesn't do what I want? What if it never happens? It will be the end of the world!*

Like Yeshua's example of bread at a feast, we can grow afraid to partake. We can become unable to truly live life for fear of what might happen, what could happen, what might not happen. We can shut down and shut away, keeping ourselves and our world within very limited boundaries we feel are *safe.*

Looking back across our lives is a major key to directing our minds away from suffering as our progress unfolds. When have we ever been abandoned? When has everything crashed and nothing worked out? When have we been doomed and died, losing everything? If we are still alive, none of these has ever happened, have they?

Everything in this universe is made of the same energy. The energy of God is all and is in all. It never runs out. It is never in a state of lack or in danger of becoming empty.

We are a part of this universe, and *are* this universe. We are made of the exact same energy everything else is made of — how can we ever be separated? We are a part of God and are God — how can we ever be separated?

As I write this, I have just turned forty-one years old. Although it may or may not be as bad as other people's experiences, I've been through winters, through deserts, through darkness, and through doubts, yet looking back, I see clearly that I've never been abandoned. Although it may or may not be as good as other people's experiences, I've been through springtimes, through rainforests, through light, and through hope, yet even in these, I've never been alone. I have always been taken care of, always been provided for, no matter what, even in times I had no idea where the next dollar or meal would come from. Sometimes things have turned out okay in big ways, sometimes they've been all right in small ways, but always in ways—perfect ways, in perfect times. Because of these experiences, and maybe because of my age and amount of life experience I now have under my belt to look back on, I am able to feel and hold to a solid trust and faith as I look forward. I feel no fear or worry of the unknown variables that may or may not happen in the future. Whatever happens, I see and know now that everything will always have a way to come, pass, and move on. *All things naturally arise, rush against each other playfully, and then subside.*

Everything will always be okay, even when our minds feel otherwise in the moment. Everything may be changed, but it will always be okay. Change does not equal doom.

I have reached a point in life where I refuse to let fear steal my peace of mind. I have realized I can no longer afford to allow it to rob me of my happiness and joy. Without peace of mind, I can't function, I can't think straight, I have no light.

Everything is what it is until it is what it's not, then it will simply be, until it's simply not.

YESHUA FINISHED BLESSING ALL his friends, redressed, and rejoined them at the table. *Things are about to become difficult for all of you,* he said. *You are about to be thrown for a loop and have to try to deal with things you'd rather not. Things will be how you wish they were not, and this is how your mind generates suffering. I do not wish for you to suffer.* They looked around at each other worriedly, the worst of their discussions and speculations at what was happening here seemed about to come true. *I'm going to tell you these things now so you will remember them again after they've happened, and hopefully it will help you in the aftermath.*

Quickly wiping a tear from the corner of his eye, Yeshua continued. *One of you here will betray me, and –* Peter, his most aggressive friend interrupted him immediately with *What! I know it's not me! I will fight to the death for you, Yeshua! Yes! I would gladly die for you!*

Yeshua placed his hand on Peter's hand softly and smiled. *No, it is not you, but you do need to know that before the rooster crows in the morning you will have denied knowing me not once, not twice, but three times.*

Impossible. Peter bellowed, offended and angry.

Yeshua merely embraced him in a hug, holding him for long moments as the others continued to look at each other in confusion, not understanding what was going on.

Still, one who has shared my bread, my life, will turn against me tonight. I will be with you only a little longer he said as he turned toward another of his friends. *Judas,* he said gently, *go and do what you must.*

Judas stood up from the table suddenly, his face a mixture of horror and anger. Yeshua held his gaze tenderly, fighting tears himself. *Quickly,* he urged.

Judas turned and ran into the night, and Yeshua sighed

heavily and shook as he leaned against the wall. *Now there is no turning back* he whispered. *Now I know it will happen.*

Raising his voice to all still in the room, he said *Love one another! Promise me! Love everyone the way that I have loved you! Love even those who do things you do not understand — there is always a reason, always a cause, though it may be buried deeper than any man can see. God knows, and that soul knows, and that is business between God and that soul.*

Where I am going, you cannot follow yet, but one day, you will be able to follow, and you will meet me there again.

Now more confused than ever, and alarmed as well, his friends asked *What? Where are you going that we can't follow? How can we come if we don't know the way?*

Yeshua replied, *I have already shown you the way — I have been living the way, I have been living the truth, I have been living the life. There is no other way to the energy of God but to love. There is no other way to become the energy of God but to become living, breathing Love walking in this place. Anyone who recognizes the example I have been for you and follows in my footsteps will find me and will become me. They will do all these things and more, as they will be here, and I am going away.*

You will never be alone: after I have gone, if you do not become lost in despair, and if you remember me and remember who you are, you will find within you an advocate — a help that has been with you all along. This spirit of truth leads you and guide you from within, where the world cannot see, where the world cannot touch, and you will realize that it is this same energy that has led me. You will once again find me there, and you will know I have only dissolved into the energy of God, and you will see that I was always the energy of God, and you will know that you are also the energy of God, and that we are eternally one. You will see that I still live, and that you also will still live beyond your own time to leave.

I wish to leave you with peace – a peace that defies all understanding. Do not let your minds be troubled; do not let your minds lead you into suffering. Difficulties are only for a moment. When a woman is giving birth, she has sorrow because her hour has come and there is much suffering, but when she has delivered the baby, she no longer remembers the anguish, because of the overwhelming joy that a human being has been born into the world. So also your sorrows and sufferings will come and go, and you will find the joy on the other side of them – joy that no one can take away from you.

Fear has no place with me or with you.

Love has every place with me and with you.

And there is no greater love than to lay down one's life for one's friends.

Continue on, and love your friends; everyone is your friend.

The time has now come for me to leave, or otherwise you will not learn to communicate with the energy of God for yourself. You know the way, now you must choose to practice it for yourselves. You will recognize the energy because it will be in line with all I have taught you and demonstrated to you. Anything that contradicts this Way is not of God, and anything that confirms and follows this way of love, this spirit of truth, is of God, wherever it may be found.

Then the human Yeshua, overcome with emotions for all that was about to happen, sighed deeply, raised his eyes to the heavens, and began to pray. *The hour has now come. May all I have shown and taught these here with me truly guide them into the oneness that is the energy of God and eternal life. May they come to know and see these things for themselves on their own, in all their comings and goings of daily life. It has been my aim to demonstrate to them and all who I've come into contact with the power of love, the true reality of God. I have done all I can to show the Way, and now it will be up to them.*

I pray for all those who have believed me and are trying to become love in this place, and I pray for all who have not believed me, who reject the living water of life that is found in loving and serving others, no matter the cost. May all beings come to know they come from love and are returning to love.

I pray that all those who choose to continue in love may have the strength to remain steady even as those who reject me now will continue to reject those who follow in my footsteps. I do not ask that they be taken from this world, for this world needs their light, but that they may find the power to overcome the sufferings in their minds. May they have minds of hope and light, finding the love in all things. May they find the advocate and guide within their own hearts. May they remember the oneness they came from. Even though they may walk through periods of darkness, may they fear nothing. May they be able to sit at their table and enjoy their feast, fully partaking of the bread and the wine, in remembrance of who they are. May they hold in their own hearts these three things: trust, hope, and love – and the most important of these is love.

I pray for all those who will take up this mission from this time forward as the Way is passed from one to another – may it spread like wildfire raging out of control! I have done all I have done, and do what I now do for the sake of all who are one with us, and there is not one who is not a part of us.

Now I have shown them everything love is, and I will continue to show them, right up to the very end. As difficult as it will be, I see there can be no other way. May it benefit all these who have been with me, and all who are yet to come, that we may all be fully together once again in the Kingdom that is the eternal foundation of all things!

Focusing on and thinking about others is another way to direct our minds from stewing in suffering. Praying for others can be as simple as sending them well-wishing energy and positive vibes. We are unable to stay in a dark pit when we focus on others and not only on ourselves — we do not deny ourselves, we do not avoid addressing our own issues and the inner work we require for our own mental, emotional, and physical health, but we remember we are not the only ones in this world, and that our problems are not the vast be-all-end-all they may feel like in the moment.

When we focus our minds on the positive, our body and attitude follow, and it is the same when we focus our minds on the negative.

Pray for others.

Bless others — outdo each other in the miracle of blessing each other! The miracle is that blessing others brings the blessing back on ourselves in time, and suffering is alleviated both in the moment and in the future, for both ourselves and others.

Breathe deeply when you realize you are processing through something. The breath of life and oxygen cycled through our body is designed to clear and move energy along — this is why our bodies naturally inhale deeply and begin sighing when we are going through something or dealing with something. Our instincts know what to do, even without our conscious direction.

Yeshua countered the anxiousness he felt with praying for others, and with looking forward to all he hoped the future would hold, intentionally choosing to give his energy to these things instead of to darker thoughts of suffering.

His mission was to demonstrate love in all its forms as a way of life, wherever it was needed, to all those who needed it, no matter their caste and status.

Now there was only one thing left that would nail the message of his mission home, and show them all what true love has the power to do.

Catch the bird of heaven,
Lock him in a cage of gold.
Look again tomorrow,
And he will be gone

Lock him in religion,
Gold and frankincense and myrrh
Carry to his prison,
But he will be gone

All the things that man has made
Cannot hold him anymore –
Still the bird is flying
As before[11]

DEATH

A WAY OF LOVE

WHAT IF ALL WE do and all we work toward, all we march for and all we fight for in our lives never comes to be in our own lifetime? We spend enormous amounts of energy and time and money shaping our visions and forming our plans, setting the things into motion we hope will guide our lives, our families, our communities, our cities, and our nations to that vision — and this is good; we would not be truly living if we were not chasing dreams. Without a vision in the distance, without a dream for the future, our day jobs that pay the bills and provide for our families would be endlessly monotonous and pointless, sucking the life out of us, eight-hour chunks at a time. Without a hope for what is to come, even all the effort and toil we put into raising our families would become depressing and exhausting.

But what if, even when everything seems to go perfectly according to the plans we set in place — and we are able to avoid all suffering that can come for our minds as we chase after these visions—what if all our best efforts to create what we want to see still fall short of making it a reality? What if we end up not living long enough to finish setting our plan into action completely? As I write this, one of my coworkers passed away suddenly and without warning this very week, shocking us all with a jolt of reality. He was always a strong, hard worker, hadn't been sick at all, and had just turned sixty-three last week. He was simply at work and fine one day, then gone the next day. What will happen to all he had planned?

Ultimately, we have no control of what happens, and cannot control anything. We may manage to manipulate and guide some things to fit our desires and hopes for a time, but deep inside us, there is an awareness that everything everywhere will eventually be out of our hands and entrusted to someone else. What will those who come after us do when we've moved on? We can't see what our children and grandchildren are going to do with what we pass down to them, what we set up for them and leave for them. What if those who come behind us care nothing about what we value? What if they don't understand or don't respect what we've done and why we've done it? What if they throw it all away for whatever in-the-moment whim they have? Will everything we've done be for nothing? The tug-of-war in our minds is enough to make us want to flip tables over or curse trees and make them shrivel—outward, visible signs of the storm raging inside our heartache and desire to maintain control of everything.

Every pathway has its own way of acknowledging death and other realizations of impermanence, acknowledging that things are only things for a limited time before returning to the way they were before. The Christian Bible has numerous comparisons to our human lives being as dust, as grass, as flowers that bloom for a little while, then fade away. In the Hindu *Katha Upanishad*, Death offers a young man many descendants, vast wealth, mighty kingdoms, gorgeous women, and any pleasure the young man could dream up, but the wise young man replies *These things only endure until tomorrow, O Destroyer of Life, and the pleasures they give wear out the senses – keep your chariots and horses, keep dance and song for yourself! How can anyone desire wealth, O Death, when they have seen your face? How can I who am subject to decay and death, and knowing well the vanity of the flesh, wish for things that quickly fade away?* The young man impresses Death so much that Death then begins teaching the young man even more about the Way of the wise. The *Tibetan Book of the Dead* calls out to us *Are you oblivious to the sufferings of birth, old age, sickness, and death?* then immediately reminds us *There is no guarantee you will survive even past this very day. Therefore, the time has come to develop perseverance in your practice, for in this very moment you could achieve all you came to this place to do.*

If there is no guarantee that whatever we do will last and not be undone by those who follow, should we simply stop trying so hard, stop caring about things so much, and just do whatever we want without a second thought about cause and effect or any long-term goal at all?

Yeshua had to have been feeling these same things as his final hours closed in around him – he actually *knew* when his time was coming, reading and sensing it in the environment around him: the energy of God communicating to him. His humanness had to be fighting the fear that all he'd done was for nothing, that nothing would change, that none of the seeds he'd planted would sprout into the kingdom he envisioned and knew was possible. He knew the instant he entered the city that the people still did not understand his message or his mission. That realization and sadness he had carried with him all week came to a head that night as he and his friends went out to the gardens after dinner, one of Yeshua's favorite spots where they had had many of their discussions and interactions.

Drowsy from the feast they had just shared, Yeshua's friends began to doze off and fall asleep as Yeshua paced the pathways of the garden in agony. *Is this the way — is this really the only way? I have taught and shown everyone everything about the energy of God and made it known and seen in this physical world. I have shown them all the Way and still they do not understand, still they look for an outward king and want to make me that king or shape their religion around me. I have held true to all my messages of peace and love, despite so many tests and traps. I have both prevented and escaped previous attempts on my life in front of their own eyes, and still they doubt the power of my message — even when they saw me thrown off a cliff and survive unharmed! Yet this cannot continue forever. They just expect me to continue escaping death and continue being their shepherd, their guide and example in loving as our Father does. They don't want to do it themselves — they aren't ready to do it themselves yet! They only want someone else to come and do these things for them. They expect me to fight if it comes to it, but they still don't understand that the essence of love is the lack of violence and harm in any way, zero discrimination and judgment — a blindness to any perceived difference between us and them at all! If I allow my life to be taken to demonstrate to them once and for all how deep the commitment to love and nonviolence must be, will they get it? Will they understand then? Will they begin to walk in their own power — the same power from the Father I have? I fear they will not! No — they will run away and scatter in all directions!*

Oh, my soul, is there any other way – any other way at all? I can't do this. I need to stay with them longer! Yet more than just loving others fiercely, they need to understand that death is not the end they think it is. They fight and wrestle for control because they fear death and believe this life is the only life and that it must be fought for regardless the cost, but the cost of all violence and hatred is far greater than the changing of clothes that death is.

Sigh

I can feel no other way. They are not ready, but the time has come. This is the very reason I do this work. I must lay aside this life to show them the full extent of The Way. I will do it, not for my own benefit, but for their benefit, that they may all become the energy of God. And then I will show them, too, that death is not the end of life as they fear.

Voices and footsteps coming through the bushes and trees interrupted Yeshua's prayers and inner debate. Soldiers carrying torches and lanterns and swords and clubs came into view and stopped when they saw Yeshua standing beside a group of people lying still on the ground. *Oh God – has he killed them all? They were right, this man is dangerous!* Several priests from the temple pushed through then and stopped next to the soldiers. In the middle of the priests was Yeshua's friend, Judas.

They all stared at each other for a few moments, until Yeshua broke the silence with a gentle *Who are you looking for?*

One of the soldiers answered loudly *Yeshua of Nazareth! Do you know the man with this name?* Yeshua's friends woke then and scrambled to their feet in alarm.

Yeshua said, *I am he.*

The crowd tensed and took a step back, looking at Judas beside them. Judas slowly came forward and stood face to face with Yeshua. *My master,* he said as he kissed Yeshua's cheek in greeting. Knowing the greeting was a confirmation signal to the soldiers, Yeshua smiled sadly as his eyes met and held Judas' eyes. *My friend,* he said, *I know you have done what you thought to be best.*

The soldiers came close and grabbed Yeshua, pulling him to the ground as the priests circled around. Yeshua's aggressive follower, Peter, let out a yell, drew his knife, and leaped into the fray. Grabbing one of the priests, Peter cut off the man's ear.

STOP! Yeshua bellowed from the ground. *No more of this! Put your swords away! Those who take up the sword will die by the sword, and I want no violence here! I want no one to be harmed!* Then Yeshua reached over and healed the man's ear.

Everyone present froze at the unexpected outburst and the miraculous healing. They had all seen the man's ear cut — now it was fine! How did he do that? *Yes!* Judas thought as a grin begin to spread across his face. *The plan to force his hand is working! He's going to take up his throne now! I knew it! We're saved!*

Yeshua broke the hesitant tension by speaking to his friends. *I have accepted the cup our Father has offered me. There is no other way. I have entered into union with the Way, and must continue following these things. I am married to it now. Do not fight or resist on my behalf — I could escape this situation as easily as the other attempts on my life, but then how would these priests' prophecies be fulfilled? Soon understanding will dawn on them as they read the ancient texts once more, and they will know they have seen these things with their own eyes, done these things with their own hands — yet there is no blame for any of them, or for any of you. Each one acts as they feel is the best way, and there is a bigger purpose at work. This is not the fulfillment you imagine, the result that you seek, but it is the way that it is.*

Turning to the band of men who came for him, Yeshua continued. *Have you come as if I am a thief or a criminal who must be captured so violently? I have been right beside you openly in the temples and village squares every day – why did you not take me then? Why have you waited for this secret place, in the middle of the night? Do what you must do with me, but leave my friends unharmed.*

Ashamed then at Yeshua's truthful observation, the priests shouted in anger to bring Yeshua to the house of Caiaphas, the high priest, for holding until daybreak. All but two of his friends turned then and ran in every direction as the soldiers hauled Yeshua to his feet and began taking him away.

The two friends who followed along behind the band of men were John, who was the most devoted to Yeshua, and Peter, who kept thinking of how Yeshua had said he would reject Yeshua three times, and was still angrily determined to prove his manliness and strength, to show that Yeshua had been wrong about him.

When the group arrived at the high priest's gates and went inside, John was recognized by the guards and known to have a good reputation and was allowed inside with the crowd, but Peter was known for his rowdy reputation and was not allowed in. Something major was clearly going down here tonight, and the guards were not about to let any more trouble than necessary disturb the situation. *Don't worry,* John whispered to him, *I'll find someone and vouch for you – stay here, I'll be right back.*

John returned with the woman in charge of the guards and gate and said, *This is my friend who came with me, please let him come in, too.* The woman looked Peter up and down. *Even someone like you is a follower of the one they arrested tonight?* Peter shook his head quickly and said *No, I'm not, I only came with John to see what's going on.* The woman grunted but stepped aside. *I don't want any trouble,* she said. *It's a cold night; we've built a fire in the courtyard you're welcome to warm yourself at.*

Grateful, Peter went to the fire while John went to find where they'd taken Yeshua. Suddenly, one of the other men standing close to the fire said, *Hey! You're one of that man's followers, aren't you?* Peter's mouth dropped open in panic. *No! I'm not—I've never even seen him before!* Immediately another standing there took a closer look at Peter. *Yes, you are!* he said. *I was in the gardens with the other soldiers tonight, and I definitely saw you there!*

NO, I WASN'T! Peter yelled. *I'm telling you, I don't even know him!!*

A rooster crowed as the people around the fire took a step back in surprise at Peter's outburst. Peter looked wildly at each of them, then turned and ran back out of the gates into the breaking dawn, wailing *What have I done? O, what have I done?*

Everything Yeshua had predicted earlier that night had happened exactly as he said. Judas had betrayed him, turning him over to those willing to kill him in fear of losing their own importance. Peter, who had argued and insisted that he was the one above all the others ready to fight for and die for Yeshua, had denied even knowing Yeshua—much less being a direct student of him—three times, to save his own skin in the fear that he would be arrested as well. The scheme the priests had been plotting for a long time was now being put into action, and he was about to die.

Knowing all these things, how could Yeshua not have wrestled with wondering what would happen to all he'd worked towards? How could he even find the strength to continue to the end, knowing the possibility that every single one of his followers may simply return back to the lives they had before they met him, never doing anything else to cultivate the kingdom at all?

He loved them.

He loved them despite anything they had done or would do.

Love is when you know things like this, and choose to love anyway.

Love is when you know it may all be for nothing, and choose to do it anyway.

There is an old Zen proverb that says *Before enlightenment: chop wood, carry water. After enlightenment: chop wood, carry water.* We often have grandiose, romantic ideas that when we reach a certain turning point, like enlightenment or finding love or discovering our purpose in life, there will be a dramatic change to everything—our daily life will be magically and vastly changed. Yet the reality is that life continues to go on and on, no different or more able to be controlled than it was before. We are still walking into the unknown, out of control, every minute of the day. We still have to keep taking care of the same daily chores we had to before, chopping wood, carrying water.

What *is* changed is internal, rather than external. What is changed at turning points and mountain summits we've reached in our lives is the way we view and respond to the daily gifts that life brings to our doorstep. What is changed is our ability to continue onward, with a strength, and a grace, and a peace that surpasses all logical understanding.

As Yeshua was led through his morning on that last day, he was able to hold his focus on the love, on the purpose, on the future goal he hoped would sprout and flourish, and this gave him the strength, patience, and peace to accept the suffering he was put through.

Once daylight fully broke, the priests and officials spent most of the morning shuffling Yeshua around from court to court, none of them wanting the responsibility of this conflict on their hands. They examined him, interrogated him, put him through mock trials, and physically beat and abused him, trying to get a reaction and a rise out of him before sending him on to the next official, saying, *I find nothing wrong with this man – besides, he's really from your jurisdiction, isn't he? This is not my problem.*

And through it all, Yeshua, the same one who had cleared out temple courtyards at least twice by dumping over tables and smashing products for sale, remained calm and nonviolent. His simple answers to the questions barked at him only conveyed and reinforced his commitment to the energy of God: love, peace, unity, and healing.

Knowing how to manipulate the reluctant officials, the priests quickly suggested to them that perhaps they should contact the king directly and let him know just how much the officials were incapable of performing their jobs and maintaining control of their region. So at last, in the face of their fears of being removed from office and the threat of losing their powers and reputations, they executed Yeshua anyway, nailing him to a wooden cross alongside a couple of criminals they were about to execute anyway.

Yeshua maintained a blameless example, even to the point of his death, so that all would know they had wrongly accused and murdered an innocent man.

Yeshua had chosen the path of being a light in this place, of being the energy of God in this place, and remained committed to that conviction to the end, no matter what it cost, illustrating to those watching and all who would hear about it afterward – including us, over two thousand years later – what was possible for everyone, as well as what strength it would sometimes require.

The more we choose to live our lives as light-bringers, the more apparent the contrast and conflict between ourselves and those who are not committed to being lights will become. The more we cultivate into our lives the habits and lifestyles of being a light, the easier the tendency is for our minds to slip into frustration and impatience with things that contrast or clash with these. Patience is of the highest importance for us to practice, so that we may watch for and guard against this. One of the Buddhist bodhisattva vows is a vow to remain present in this place even after realizing oneness with the energy of God, so that they may assist others still walking the path, and demonstrate the Way to others by living it openly among those others. Any teacher is a teacher because they already know the material they're teaching to others. Would it be acceptable for a teacher to resent their students, or berate and scoff at them for not already knowing the material themselves?

As a human, I often catch my initial reaction being anger and impatience when I see others tripping into cycles I know are harmful, and falling for mind traps that no longer affect me. *Why can't they just see how destructive this is and stop it?* I think.

Things I've been through are obvious to me because I've been through them, and it's so easy for this human mind to begin judging and criticizing others who may still be in the process of learning. I find myself losing patience with them and growing more restless around them instead of being more present for them, and more able to meet their needs. It's a daily practice of mindfulness to try again fresh each new day.

Another thing I'm aware of in my own life is that, as patient a person I am in many areas, I do have a very low threshold for things like poor customer service, unprofessional behavior in a place of business, or wait-staff that is inattentive to the needs of my family when we chose *their* establishment to eat at out of the dozens of local options we had available to us. It's something I have to personally be mindful about. I must consciously work at gifting more grace in situations like these—it's what the energy of God would do, plus there's no way I can know what they may be experiencing in that moment. Maybe they've just lost a loved one and are trying their best to cope, or maybe they're not feeling well but have no sick leave benefits and can't afford to miss any work, or maybe they have a disability that's unable to be seen outwardly. There are limitless possibilities I am unaware of, and they are most likely doing the absolute best they can under their current circumstances. My responsibility is not to find out what the deal is and fix it, nor is it to react personally and defensively; my only responsibility is to open and maintain a space for the energy of God—the energy of love—to channel through my presence, and be present in the situation.

The very task of raising a family is often a difficult and intense test, a constant practice ground for seeking to find the most loving and graceful way in every situation. Anyone who is a parent understands what a miracle—and what a struggle— it is to continue loving others, and to keep giving to others with an insane generosity, even when it is not deserved. Most children and teenagers will mooch everything and contribute nothing, resisting every bit of instruction and advice simply for the sake of resisting it. Do we turn our backs and ignore them with a silent treatment of judgment? No, like Yeshua, we continue loving them and giving to them and guiding them, having faith that it is somehow sinking in, and that one day the wisdom we have sown in them will take root and grow, reappearing in perfect time.

We have to trust.

We have to trust in the same way Yeshua had to trust as he allowed himself to become the ultimate example of pure love. Yeshua could have easily just said *Forget it: you don't get it, none of you understand – I'm not going to put up with this!* and walked away to live out the rest of his life in peace and quiet.

But what sort of love claims to be unconditional and dedicated, then quits and leaves when things get not-so-pleasant? Whether devoted to a person or a cause or a movement, pure love remains committed to the end, unless it is causing harm to itself or others.

If we were to literally imagine God as a person, being a parent is the closest thing to how it feels to do everything we can for wild, unexperienced, and unkempt children – and how it is to keep loving them with everything we are anyway.

The energy of God is long-sighted, patient, trusting that all will work out, trusting that all will find a way to work out, no matter what happens. There is no fear about what will happen. There is only complete freedom. There is desire for the best and most loving way to be chosen, but there is no attachment to controlling the situation to try to make that best happen, only complete freedom and understanding that all things must come to their own time naturally.

The energy of God is love, joy, and peace; the energy of God is love, joy, and peace even when it's undeserved and unearned.

As a member of a family, I have the perfect opportunity to practice embodying these Godly things, but while I'm in this human form trying hard to gracefully be all these things to my wife and children, I find over and over again that I can't.

I'm human.

I'm messy.

I get tired and cranky.

I get sick and lose patience.

I can't be consistently perfect, loving recklessly, loving unconditionally, twenty-four seven.

But guess what?

Nothing has happened.

I've not been struck down with lightning from the sky or cursed with an incurable disease in punishment for not being perfect.

What I *have* been given is a new day, over and over, to go again.

It's okay.

It's *not* okay to just dismiss the times we do fall short as no big deal and keep doing the same thing without any sincere effort to do otherwise; it *is* okay because we keep getting back up and starting each new day over, trying our best again and again.

That's all that's expected of us—all with zero condemnation.

We do our absolute best, keeping our eyes fixed on our goal, keeping ourselves surrounded by things that influence and reinforce our aim, and we keep going.

And *that* is perfect.

THIS HOLY WEEK SEEMED to now be at an end with the murder of Yeshua and his hasty burial. The priests and religious leaders thought they'd won and successfully pulled off their scheme to rid themselves of Yeshua, the Roman officials thought it was all over and they'd escaped their worst fears and upheld their ongoing *Operation Job Security* record, and Yeshua's followers sat around in shock and confusion, wondering why he was lying in a tomb instead of sitting on the throne.

The day after his crucifixion was their holy day, the Sabbath. Nobody came to visit the tomb he had been laid in that day, so they would not be accused of breaking the strict and legalistic laws that allowed no work or exertion of any form on the Sabbath, the day of rest. None of them wanted to risk being arrested or murdered as well.

At the crack of dawn the next day, though, Mary the Magdalene, who had been a close friend and follower of Yeshua since he had saved her life, went to the tomb by herself, and was surprised to find the giant stone that had been rolled to cover the opening of the cave had been rolled away again! This was so unexpected that she turned and ran to John's house to tell him. When she arrived, she found Peter sitting and talking with John, looking extremely distraught. *I've just been to the tomb where they laid Yeshua!* she cried. *The stone has been rolled from the entrance!* The two men leaped to their feet. *What! Are you sure? Did you look inside?* Mary's mouth dropped open. *No! I didn't even think to – I ran straight here!*

Peter and John took off running to the tomb. John arrived first, bent to look inside, saw the linen Yeshua's body had been wrapped in lying there, and collapsed to the ground sobbing, *He's gone! They've taken him!*

When Peter arrived, he ran straight into the tomb without hesitating, still bold, even in his sorrow and angst. He saw the linens still laying spread out in place as if holding a body that was no longer there, but found the smaller head cloth separate from the rest and folded neatly in the corner. *Wha – ? This doesn't make sense... They moved him, yet left his wrappings? No one would do such an unclean thing!*

John stumbled in then to see what Peter was talking about. He sank to the floor again as realization struck him. *Nobody's taken him,* he whispered in awe. Peter stared at him. *Do you remember when he told us he was about to go away? Do you remember he said 'Let no fear overtake you — you will find me again; you will see that I still live'?*

He's done it... He has continued to live beyond death!

And Peter wept.

On the day I die,
when I'm being carried toward the grave,

Don't weep.

Don't say, He's gone! He's gone.

Death has nothing to do with going away.

The sun sets and the moon sets, but they're not gone.

Death is a coming together.

The tomb looks like a prison,
but it's really release into union...[12]

AFTERLIFE

FRUIT OF THE SPIRIT

THERE IS ONE LAST beautiful example of the energy of God left behind for us by Yeshua of Nazareth in Galilee.

Peter, who had been the one to carry his knife and sword with him always, ready to fight a physical battle for Yeshua's honor, and who had so aggressively insisted he would in a heartbeat go as far as death for Yeshua, had turned out to be the one who not only ran away when things got real, but also the only one who actually denied to others he had anything to do with Yeshua in the first place — three times!

Any one of us can imagine the anguish, shame, and inner torment he experienced in the days after Yeshua's death, how utterly humbling to have been the one to brag so extensively about his convictions, yet crumble to the extreme opposite when it came down to it. Most of us can relate to similar situations. All of Yeshua's friends had to have known about what he did, the word had to have spread quickly, yet still Peter did not stay in hiding: as early as the third day after it happened, he had come to John—the only one who did not run away—and was confessing and discussing his behavior when Mary rushed in with the news about the tomb. Peter had true bravery after all to come back after what he did—he could have easily booked passage on the next ship out of town and never been seen again.

Slipping up or messing up never has to mean all is lost and doomed and unforgivable for any of us. John must have been such a grace-filled and loving man to know this and to embrace Peter without condition. I believe John was the one who *got it* the most, the first of them all to truly embody the energy of God in the ways Yeshua demonstrated.

How many of us are able to demonstrate the energy of God in such an unconditional way to those around us who are in the middle of their own struggles? The struggles of others seem to be even more visible in this time thanks to the internet and social media; anyone can post their thoughts and feelings and status online for all the world to see and know. It's so easy to not want to be bothered by things like this, or to judge and criticize others for struggling. How many of us can simply sit down with them and listen to them, gifting them with an outlet for the excess energy to find a way out of their system and free up their space for light to enter again? One would think that having the entire world connected via the internet would make things less lonely and more compassionate, but somehow the opposite is true.

After life happens, life continues. Whether it's after experiencing a major loss or setback, or after physical death, everyone must continue, and this is the place Yeshua's friends and followers found themselves in.

As they all struggled to process these things and figure out where they now stood, and who they now were, and how in the world they were going to keep chopping wood and carrying water, Peter's struggle was the greatest. That night had to be replaying over and over in his mind, beating himself up over his cowardly behavior. I'm sure every time he closed his eyes, he saw again the fire pit he had been trying to warm up next to, saw the faces of those who recognized him as one of Yeshua's followers, heard his own screaming and running away into the night.

Yet even this inner torture was not enough at first for him to be instantly all-in again. He had swallowed pride and been accepted to continue spending time with the others, which graciously helped him begin his healing process, but several times the sacred texts tell how Yeshua had miraculously manifested in front of the group behind locked doors after his death, and Peter was clearly present at these times, yet apparently remained quiet in the back of the room, hiding in the corner, still unable to face Yeshua directly.

How human!

Any time any one of us are working at changing a habit or processing through an experience or overcoming an addiction, there is no one able to accomplish this overnight. There is no switch to be toggled to turn the thing off or on; it is always an ongoing process, often a progress of two steps forward, one step back. Our human minds—these astounding machines in our head that run on strict programming and routine—need to ease into a new thing slowly.

Yet even these times ate away at Peter's insides. *Why, O why can I not just talk to him? Why can't I just get it over with? I've got to just face what I did! He knew about it beforehand, after all – he's the one who told me about it before it even happened!*

Every one of us can go one of two ways with our processes like this: we can give up entirely and stop trying, or we can use the frustration of setbacks as fuel to propel ourselves and our spirits forward and cover the last distance to the finish line, arriving at the place we want to be.

And Peter was able to reach the place where he had had enough.

It had been some time since Yeshua had manifested to the group, and most of them had begun to accept that he was done appearing to them now; they were on their own and trying to figure out how to continue spreading The Way.

Then one evening, some of the followers, including Peter and John, went out in their boat to spend the night fishing, which was one of their main sources of income. They cast their nets and reeled them in over and over all night, but caught nothing. When the sky began to lighten in the east, they decided to give up in frustration and come back to shore.

As they grew close to shore, a man standing on the beach called out to them, *Hello out there! Have you caught any fish to sell?* They yelled back, *No, brother, we had no luck this night.* The man called out again, *Try one more time, and cast your net on the right side of your boat, right where you are!* Probably thinking the man was an old expert fisherman and marketplace merchant who knew something about the spot they didn't know, they did as he instructed. The net was suddenly full of so many fish they could barely lift it back onto the boat!

Suddenly, the energy of God that John had become recognized the energy of God standing on the beach. *It's Yeshua!!* he yelled.

Peter's head whipped around so quickly it's a wonder he didn't give himself whiplash.

Peter dropped his part of the net they were trying to haul aboard and threw himself into the sea, thrashing and splashing wildly in a frantic swim to shore.

Peter came face to face with Yeshua and collapsed to the sand, weeping uncontrollably.

Yeshua lifted Peter and just held him as the others made their way to shore in the boat. When they all arrived, they noticed a fire pit had been lit nearby. *Come, my friends,* Yeshua said, *Warm yourselves at the fire, and bring some of the fish you've caught for breakfast.*

Can you imagine the thoughts going through Peter's mind as they sat at the same sort of fire he had been next to when he had denied he was involved with Yeshua? It was even about the same crack-of-dawn hour of the day! Was Yeshua doing this to torture and punish him?

The group cooked and ate the breakfast together with Yeshua in silence, none of them sure of what to say or do, but overjoyed to simply be in his presence again. As Yeshua met each of their eyes comfortably, including Peter's, and smiled brightly at them all, Peter slowly began to realize there was no judgmental or punitive intention in Yeshua's actions.

When they had finished breakfast, and they were all still sitting around the early morning fire, Yeshua finally spoke.

Peter, do you love me?

Having been about to burst, dying to say something—anything—Peter immediately blurted out, *Yes! You know I love you!*

Feed my people, Yeshua replied.

Peter had been puzzling on that for a few minutes when

Yeshua spoke again.

Peter, do you love me?

Looking back up in confusion, Peter said again, *Yes... You know I love you...*

Take care of my people.

Then Yeshua asked a third time, *Peter, do you love me?*

A moan of despair escaped Peter. *He doesn't believe me! I really have gone too far – I am doomed after all!* he thought, but desperately said aloud, *Yes! You know everything; you know I really do love you!*

Yeshua smiled. *Feed my people.*

Understanding began to dawn in Peter's mind as Yeshua stood up from the fire. *Follow me,* he said.

Without hesitation, Peter jumped up and began to walk with Yeshua, but then paused and looked back. *What about the others?*

What about them? Yeshua replied. *What does it matter to you what others do? You choose your way for you.*

Peter instantly started walking again.

Back there... it wasn't that you didn't believe me, was it? You were forgiving, giving three opportunities to reclaim three offenses.

Yeshua nodded.

Peter released a sob of relief and grief.

But... what if I had denied seven times? Would you still have been able to forgive seven times?

Yeshua stopped and smiled broadly. *Seven thousand and seven times.*

Peter collapsed to the beach once again, overwhelmed by such unconditional acceptance and love. Yeshua gently laid his hand on Peter's head. *Go, and do as I have done.*

The energy of God keeps no tally of offenses. As the energy

of God, we continue loving and serving those in need regardless of what they have done to us or to others. We understand and keep in mind that each one is in their own world, fighting their own internal battles, processing their own personal struggles, and nothing they say or do while projecting on to us really has anything to do with us personally at all. When we do not take things as personal offenses, we are able to love unconditionally, as Yeshua.

A fight against injustice is often ignited by an anger or an outrage, but a fight against injustice cannot continue to be held in this state or it will eventually become unjust itself. The anger or rage is to spark us into action, but must be let go of once we are in motion. To continue to chase after a thing in anger will not allow the wiggle room — the grace — needed for the desired change to happen. Where there is no forgiveness, there can be no permission to change; the grudge will forever be hovering overhead. The other will forever be the *other*: the ones who did *that thing* in the past.

Forgive. Release. Bless!

Allow them another try, as you have been graced countless tries in your own life.

Life in this physical existence naturally gifts us with do-over after do-over, presenting us with the same scenarios in multiple forms over and over. We get to try a thing again and again, with no condemnation.

After life, there is more life.

This life is unpredictable and uncontrollable. After anything in life happens, we have a choice: if it is something undesirable and *bad* to us, we have the choice to spiral down into a pit of resentment and hopelessness with it, or to take it as strengthening and use it to climb higher; if it is something desirable and *good* to us, we have the choice to take it for granted and let it slip away in the belief that it will always stay that way, or appreciate it and intentionally cultivate it to grow and flourish into even greater greatness.

After Peter had crashed, died inside, and experienced such a dark night that he felt buried alive, he found an after-life, and went on to become one of the most influential leaders in the continuing work toward spreading The Way to other regions, wanting all to experience and know that a love so unconditional and gracious not only existed but was the foundation supporting all things and the key to eliminating suffering. Peter rose from his grave stronger and even more genuinely committed than he had bragged about being before. If Yeshua had said *Nope! Sorry! You turned on me, you're out; I turn my back on you!* and rejected Peter on the basis of Peter's emotion-based actions in the heat of the moment, the example and spreading of the kingdom—The Way—that Peter went on to demonstrate would have suffered and been snuffed out.

Go, and do as I have done.

The last time Yeshua's friends saw him he repeated this commission. *Go out to every land and be the energy of God. Surround everyone with the image of God – splash it on them like a water baptism. Love, serve, forgive, bless, plant seeds wherever you go, that they, too, may wake up and remember who they are, and may realize that they have come from Love and are returning to Love. Look for the kingdom of God and the most loving way in all things, and everything you need will be arranged around you naturally. And remember: I am with you forever!*

We always have everything we need. Whatever seeds we have accepted and cultivated in our lives—whether positive or negative—will always attract ways to be watered. We will always be led to people and places and things that will grow the seeds we have chosen for ourselves, the seeds we allow to shape our minds and our lives. Our eyes open to whatever our focus is around us, just as they do if we buy a purple truck, for example, and only then begin to realize just how many other purple trucks are out on the roads as well—we never noticed until it was in our field of awareness.

As the longings of our heart increase and we search for places these desires can flourish, places where we feel our spirit can breathe, we will often find that these places are not very near our own home. We want to rush off to these places where great things have happened or are happening, to be a part of them ourselves, to connect with that energy. That's beautiful and that's the pull of it, the attraction, but those places already have that—why do they need more?

What about *our* place?

What about where we already are?

What if great things were happening around us and attracting others that way?

What would it take to plant seeds that will grow that sort of energy right here?

A seed is buried—overwhelmed by this earth.

A seed dies—cracked and broken in the darkness.

A seed is touched by living water—exploded from death to life.

A seed is transformed—rearranged and rooted for rapid growth.

A seed surfaces—reaching the air, drinking the light.

We are the stripped down, rebuilt, breathing ones.

We are the energy of God.

Though we cannot think alike,
may we not love alike?

May we not be of one heart,
though we are not of one opinion?

Without a doubt,
we may.

This is how
all the children of God
may unite.[13]

TRANSLATION

KEY TO THE KINGDOM

YESHUA UNDERSTOOD THAT THE inside — the core — of a person or a system has to change in order for the whole to be truly changed. He understood that any surface-level modifications will ultimately be just that: superficial, cosmetic, eventually fading back into whatever patterns and habits exist at the foundation. He aimed his work at this core foundation, shaping and customizing everything he taught according to the audience listening to him that day, so that it could be understood and absorbed by every person, at every level.

Yeshua did not push a changed religion, or push his own religion, or push any other nation's religion. He simply looked at the environment and surroundings he found himself in, and taught ways to live as love within that existing system, knowing that the whole of the system itself would gradually re-shape over time into what its core — its root — was fed.

If Yeshua's system had been a society based on cannibalism, then he may have planted the idea-seeds that would begin steering the people's thoughts toward realizing *Maybe these are other sentient beings, just the same as we are, and we're eating them — and that's causing harm to them!* and in a natural progression over time, they could have eventually come to the decision to not eat other people.

As it was, Yeshua's society was based on four-thousand-year-old traditions that had evolved from human sacrifices of their own children to animal sacrifices of birds and lambs, but still couldn't let go of the idea the people were inherently bad and needed to make offerings and sacrifices to forces greater than themselves, to make sure they were safe and in good favor. Yeshua knew this was not the truth, and knew that the people themselves were an inseparable part of that greater force they felt and paid tribute to—not pathetic underlings to it. He also understood that they would not be able to grow past these concepts without new symbolism to replace the old symbolism in their minds. They had grown so far, but it was now time to begin taking their next step.

Look! There goes the lamb of God!

It was Peter and John and those who came to the group after Yeshua's death who finally realized the additional layer of what Yeshua had done for them: Yeshua had more than simply remained committed to love and nonviolence even in the threat of death, he had more than just laid down his life in order to prolong the lives of all his friends who would have otherwise begun to lose their lives before their time because of him—he had allowed himself to finally be murdered at the exact time of the yearly animal sacrifices so the people could put together in their minds that there had been one last sacrifice, one final offering of love. Now the people could come to the realization that the only final, once-and-for-all sacrifice *they* needed to give was the sacrifice of themselves in the same way, the offering of their own self-centered existence, to realize that *love* is The Way to good favor with the energy of God rather than the ritual killing of other living beings.

The people gradually began to understand these things, and began to swing to the center balance Yeshua had hoped for, the balance that would create the kingdom of God. Yet once again, one of our ever-present human conditions is the tendency to look outside ourselves and want someone or something out there to do our work for us, to come save us — essentially releasing us of our own responsibilities.

All during Yeshua's mission, people had already called him the *Son of God*, especially every time he healed someone or accomplished some other sort of miraculous feat. Yeshua had countered that by referring to himself to them as the *Son of Man*, trying to show them that what he had found and done, they could find and do as well. The way he referred to God as his Father was taken by them as another clue that *Son of God* really was correct, even though he showed them clearly that he meant God was everyone's father by teaching them to pray beginning with *Our Father*. When Yeshua told them *If you have seen me, you have seen the Father,* he was referring to the energy of God and Way of Love he demonstrated — not confirming to them that he *was* God.

But when people want to see or find a specific thing, they can do a remarkable job at ignoring any opposing signs and evidence in front of their eyes, and it is still the same today. During his whole mission, they refused to see anything other than that he could be the physical king they imagined overthrowing their oppressors. Even Yeshua's own cousin, John the Baptizer, who had *prepared the way* for Yeshua, and had himself baptized Yeshua, had misunderstood what was meant to happen: after a time had passed and Yeshua still hadn't assumed the throne, John sent his people to Yeshua to ask, *Well, are you or are you not the messiah we've been waiting for? Should we keep looking for another, or what?*

The Way and the kingdom is to be love.

After Yeshua was gone, the people continued working to spread The Way as Yeshua had encouraged them to do, but quickly started to swing too far in the opposite extreme. They began developing the new kingdom into just another version of the old kingdom with new kingdom imagery, full of the same sort of legalistic rules, regulations, and theologies. They once again elevated Yeshua to be fully God, even going so far as to begin teaching people that Yeshua's final sacrifice was literally the only way for people to ensure good favor with God — relying again on an outside source to rescue them instead of making their own personal final self-sacrifice and becoming love in this place right where they are, just as they are. If people didn't accept their story of Yeshua and their brand of spirituality in exactly the same way they did, they taught the people they would be cast out and doomed to judgment.

This is not the way of love at all.

It is long past time to begin swinging back into balance again.

It's time to live as the kingdom again, no matter what religion or path we connect to.

But how do we deal with others around us who push old brands of the kingdom on us? How do we participate in and thrive in a community where not everyone understands things the same way we do?

The key is in developing the ability to translate these things within ourselves. When we are committed to love and open-heartedness, we become able to convert the core of things inside ourselves, and we are then able to use the same languages and images those around us are using, understanding that we are meaning and talking about the same things, only understanding with different imagery in our own ways. When we are able to reach this level of comfort in the midst of difference, then we are truly able to love and find the most loving way in any situation, in *every* situation we find ourselves. We are able to communicate with anyone, truly listening, truly hearing, truly seeing them.

When I was away from the church and did not consider myself Christian anymore, I still loved talking to my Christian friends, and I talked to them in their own language, keeping up to date with and using their own popular catch-phrases. In my head, I meant something different, but understood it was not different. I could easily say to them, *God knows what you need before you need it and will meet your need in perfect timing* and mean inside, *The Universe is vast and unlimited and never ever leaves us in a void or a place of lack – your needs will be met, even if it's not in the exact way you expected or imagined.* I could comfortably say, *I'm praying for you, Sister* and mean, *I'm sending healing and loving energy to you because I know that you are me and I am you and your suffering is my own suffering.*

It is in ways like this that all people, all religions, all cultures, and all walks of life will be able to get along and come to an understanding of each other, and love each other, and arrive at a place of unity.

Such openness as this is the key to the Kingdom.

I'm extremely grateful I still always had these people around me, as I look back and see how this greatly helped me keep my heart open, and was definitely a crucial part of my healing process.

I came to a deeper understanding that religions are simply vehicles for expressing inner spirituality in outer, physical ways. The words and symbols and concepts that are used do not matter. We are currently in a physical existence and must filter inner experiences such as thoughts and feelings into physical expressions in order to both experience them fully and communicate them to others. The words on this page are an example of that: how would I be able to communicate my thoughts to you unless I translated them into some form of physical existence—this book?

Yet many people follow the motions and rules of a religion no deeper than the religion itself; no deeper spirituality is present.

The systems and governments that persecute and try to snuff out certain religions are hoping that this surface level is all the people of that religion have. They hope that if the religion itself is banned and put to an end, it will disappear, and the people will then have only their governmental system and authority to look to and depend on. They are hoping there is not a deeper spirituality behind the religious vehicle.

If your spirituality cannot survive outside a religion, then it is not true spirituality. Those who have their religion forbidden or taken away can never be stopped because the religion is only a packaging, a channel for their deeper awareness. If the religion is removed, there is plenty else in the world to become the expression—their spirituality *is* everything in the world; the entire world *is* the expression.

This is the level of love Yeshua taught.

This is the kingdom he envisioned and knew was possible: the level of seeing and knowing and understanding that all of life is only one — and that that oneness is what love is.

When this is truly realized, the compassion and nonviolence and heart-desire to serve, heal, and love are naturally lived out in every daily task.

So we translate.

We can pick up any sacred text and find within its pages the understanding to see it is the same concepts, the same love, the same energy of God our own cultural imagery relays. The translation of the text, or the language it's been converted to, or which version of that conversion we read doesn't matter — it's all only pointers, all only tools to share the heart of the message, leading us to connect to it for ourselves, in our own way.

It's not the sacred texts themselves that create the connection — that would again be mistaking the finger pointing to the moon as being the moon itself — but the pondering they inspire that causes us to connect for ourselves. In this way, we can even read and meditate on a text from a religion or path we completely do not connect with and still be led to a wide-open connection, if we are whole in ourselves and able to think for ourselves. Even fiction and entertainment can lead us to a direct connection with the energy of God if we're open to it.

When we conquer the fear of the different and the fear of the unknown, we can find that our own beliefs and path are in no way diminished, disproven, or threatened. Instead, we find they are actually enhanced and confirmed in the light of the new angle — the angle of learning about the paths and cultures of others.

I love the blue of the sky; I've always loved the blue sky.

Eventually, I discovered that the reason the sky is blue is because of the atmosphere around our planet. As light from the sun pierces the atmosphere, the specific combination of chemicals and gases in our air acts like a prism and separates the white sunlight into the full color spectrum. The blue light is the color that makes it through to our eyes more than the other colors, and therefore creates the blue tint of the sky. But gaining the knowledge of these facts did nothing to diminish my love for the blue sky — on the contrary, it makes it even more amazing and miraculous to me! How wonderful, how magnificent this place is — so complicated, yet so exact!

Learning about the environments, lives, and understandings others have will in no way harm or destroy our own environments and beliefs. We are each securely in our own environment and society, and we get to choose our paths from our own hearts, our own feelings — nobody can ever make us do anything else, and anything less will be completely inauthentic. Why does learning of another way have to mean we are throwing our own Way out with the trash? Why should we not be able to take what we have, look at it through the lens of another's way, look at it from another angle, and, if pieces of that other way touch our heart, speak to our core, and enhance our understanding of our own way, then absorb those pieces *into* our own way, shaping and molding all that moves us into what we more perfectly need to become the energy of God in this place?

There is no path or religion that is not already a patchwork quilt of multiple cultures and concepts; everything has pieces of everything else, at every level.

It's okay to update.

It's okay to revise.

It's even okay to start from scratch, if necessary!

Nothing we have today is in its first generation of invention—every single thing has been revised and improved upon as time goes on and our understanding grows.

To be so bound and locked to only one certain, black-and-white way is to wrap ourselves in chains and weights of our own making like Ebenezer Scrooge's business partner Jacob Marley in Charles Dickens' *A Christmas Carol*. In this condition, all growth has come to a halt, life is stagnant, not truly being lived, and there is no room or openness for new levels of understanding—we are dead.

We need resurrection.

The energy of God is the free-flowing, unbound, freedom to love with abandon. It cannot be captured by any set of religious rules or any other sort of regulations. It may find a partial voice and body in a religion or a concept, but it can never be completely embodied—that is impossible. Many people will try to insist there is only one overall truth, one ultimate reality, and there is, but it is so far above what our human minds are able to imagine, so far beyond what all our sciences can discover that not one flavor of our religions, not one branch of our sciences can begin to encompass its entirety. We get flashes, little bursts of insight touching the hem of it, but not the whole of it. This is what it means when the *Tao Te Ching* says that the Tao (the Way) that can be named (labeled or verbalized) is not the totality of the Way, but only a fragment of that whole Way.

But this does not mean that that ultimate reality is something distant, something *out there*, something separate from ourselves. It is around everything, in everything, and *is* everything. The *Heart Sutra* says that form is not separate from non-form (energy, Spirit), and non-form is not separate from (or even limited by) form. The Bible says that the way of the Christ *is* all and is *in* all. To think that the truth is somewhere out there and we are somewhere in here is the ultimate *us* and *them* view, and might possibly be at the root of the *us* and *them* racial and cultural problems we suffer from here.

In attempting to draw closer to this Whole, many traditions practice various rituals of *epiclesis*, each in their own way. *Epiclesis* is a Greek word meaning *invocation*, and is the invitation or the requesting of the presence of someone or something, usually a spirit or deity. The word is formed from *epi*, which means "upon, on, or at," and *klesis*, which is "prayer," as well as *kalein*, which is "to call."

In the Catholic Church, it is the calling down of the presence of the Holy Spirit to inhabit the bread and the cup, to then be consumed by those attending as a physical sign of inviting Spirit to be with them and work through them. In Buddhist traditions, it is the puja (prayer) ceremonies inviting the essence of specific Bodhisattvas and Deities to come be present in this world for the benefit and enlightenment of all living beings. In Native American tribes, it is the ceremonies and sings held to call in the participation and help of the Great Spirit in the healing, balancing, and harmony of the lives of the People.

Epiclesis is The Invitation as well as The Search.

Come, it is cried. *Be with us. Show yourself to us!*

What is perceived by human minds as a gap, a separation, is sought to be eliminated, so that communication and wisdom may then be accessed and experienced.

Yet the separation does not exist; the *epiclesis* does not change the state of any place, person, or thing, but instead seeks to direct the perception of the participant to become aware of what is already a reality—Spirit is *already* present, *already* the object, *already* a part of all things.

This is the main point Yeshua wanted everyone to understand: there is no separation, there has never been any separation, and there will never be any separation. Any perceived separation or distance is solely on our end, from our perspective, in our own belief. There is nothing we need to do, no one we need to go to, and no mediator required to connect with the energy of God. There is no application and approval process, no standard cr condition to meet first, and no test to pass.

The people were already able to connect to the energy of God all along, all on their own.

We've been able to connect to the energy of God all along.

We've had the ability ard the choice to *be* the energy of God all along—no external assistance needed.

Every time you see the word *God*, replace it with the word *Love* and read it again. Every time you hear the word *sin*, translate it to *separation* or *the things that create harmful, unloving situations and hatred and division* and listen to it again. Every time someone speaks of *the devil*, convert it to *the mind* and think on these things. Look back across your own life and look for the places these things appeared; every one of us have experienced every one of these.

Follow the leads of your heart.

Find your Way that is closest to the truth.

Find your understanding of others' truth.

Find your translation.

Find your way to love

Be that.

Make every effort
to live in peace with all the world
and to be love –

without love
you will not be able to recognize the energy of God.

See to it that no one is denied grace
and that no bitter root grows up.

You're blessed when you can show people
how to cooperate
instead of compete or fight.

That's when you discover who you really are,
and finally find your place
in God's family.[14]

POSTFACE

GOD IS A PERSON

I REALIZE THAT PIECES of this book may have seemed controversial or even sacrilegious to some — not the way you've always heard it, and maybe even touching things you were told are flat-out wrong or twisted. I hope that pieces of this book have also lifted some burdens, *set some captives free.*

These things may be the truths of it all; these things may still be missing the truth of it all. Ultimately, the details do not matter as much as the message. My hope has been only to spark internal examinations for you: go back to your beginning, start over from scratch, keep only what you feel and know in your heart is the truth, see where that leaves you, and rebuild from there.

My purpose has not been to be intentionally scandalous or rebellious, and I have absolutely no desire to create division or conflict. There is more than enough of that in this world already.

I only want to see freedom.

I only want to see peace and unity, above all. Why argue and debate and fight and nitpick over details that will always remain unprovable and unknown and up to personal preference when we can instead simply relish and live out the core of the Way together—the Love which everyone *can* indisputably agree on?

I only want to see suffering eased and dissolved. It's clear that much of our sufferings are internal and perpetuated by our own minds, even though much of it has been imposed from the world by what we've been repeatedly told about who and what we are. But we are never stuck in the patterns of the world this way; we can begin to transform our minds and renew them through loving and being loved.

It is never too late.

It becomes very dangerous trying to talk about how things *should* be, how things are *supposed* to be. It comes with the risk of boxing things back up too firmly or statically or fundamentally once again, the same way the new Way easily became the old Way in different costume and makeup. Flexibility and wiggle-room must always be present—an open mind, the *Beginner's Mind*.

I've never been able to simply accept whatever was told to me; I always wanted to research it for myself, discover for myself what was at the bottom of a thing, and make my own decisions, following what my own heart-core—connected to Spirit—spoke to me. Nothing else felt *real*.

When my ongoing process of growth and healing circled back around, and I reached the need to understand what I felt about the energy of God, it was no different. I knew beyond a doubt that *God* is the Universe, the everything of everything and everyone, but I wasn't exactly sure what that looked like here in the physical realm. How did that translate to and work with humanity?

I began by following the trail of things that clearly usher in the energy of God, the presence of God. I found God in things like strangers and enemies uniting together in a time of great need, those who had committed extreme crimes being genuinely forgiven by those who were harmed by those crimes, and those who are hated and discriminated against being defended and stood beside by others who risk rejection from their own families and friends and churches by doing so.

My search led me right back around to the most prominent example of the energy of God ever recorded, Yeshua of Nazareth. This was not a turn I expected — I had long ago written off Christianity as too harsh, too extreme, too judgmental, and certainly *not* the bearer of the energy of God that my bones knew to be true. I had been raised in the church, and had seen too much to be able to stay there.

Yet, after a time of wrestling with it, I came to the decision to embrace *Beginner's Mind* and go back to my beginning. I started by reading and studying the life of Yeshua straight through, in its entirety. I found there were many things there I had never noticed or known before, and many things *not* there that I had been told and taught were there.

And I was surprised I *did* feel the energy of God there.

I found that God *is* a person.

I found that that God-person taught that we are *all* God-people.

We are all the children of God.

What I did *not* find in the example of his life was any indication of judging, shaming, blaming, abusing, discriminating or controlling others, and no demonstration of him ever trying to convert and keep people to only himself or a religion based on himself; in every case he only loved them, showed them how to love, and then sent them back out into the world, back to their own lifestyles and religions and families, to spread and infect others with simple, holy love.

In every instance, in every encounter, Yeshua treated each and every person as an equal.

I also noticed that before he did anything for anyone, he always asked them what *they* wanted, had *them* voice and put words to their desires for themselves, prompted them and waited for them to speak their faith on their own—what *they* believed could be done.

It's always been up to us.

And, whether they were ready or not ready yet, he loved them.

He wanted each and every one of them to reach that place of ultimate Self-realization: enlightenment.

But this Self-realization is not an ego-trip self-realization as in *all about me-me-me*, as in *I must look out for me first, I must never put myself out*. This is Self-realization as in realizing *what* my self is, realizing *who* my self is, seeing that my Self *is* God.

Some would immediately say to this, *Oh, then that's an even more ultimate ego trip 'I am God! I am all powerful! Look at me!'*

But in truly finding ourselves as God, we find ourselves as everyone else, no different, no higher than anyone else. Individual ego evaporates. We begin to realize that our ego, our action, our karma really *is* perpetuated by our own hand. Being self-reliant—not relying on something else *out there* to do everything for us, not relying on and waiting for some god-figure to come save us while we sit back and do nothing—does not diminish or take away from connecting to the energy of God as some would have us believe: it actually enhances the connection to the energy of God! When we become empowered and complete in our self, we find we *are* children of God, we *are* the son of God, we *are* the daughter of God, we *are* a part of the whole, and the whole could not and would not be whole without us!

Moaning and groveling and behaving like, *Oh I'm so ashamed! I need forgiveness! I'm so powerless!* does nothing to enhance God's presence or our awareness of God. Connecting with the energy, being the energy, and channeling the energy of God is what enhances and connects us and others to God.

Removing Yeshua from the pedestal of super-divinity does not ruin everything, is not heresy or blasphemy, but rather enhances him and his message—he *was* a human, no different than us. This means that we, too, have the ability and capability to be like Yeshua and do what he did—and more. Remember Yeshua even told others, told us, *You will be able to do even greater things than I have done.* Each and every one of us has this divinity inside us.

It's what we're made of.

He has shown us the Way to resurrect from the ways of death to the Way of Life. We are not the hopeless living dead. We are merely sleeping Life!

There is no joy whatsoever in shame, in guilt, or in the fabricated joy based on the psychological idea of *I was lost and unlovable but have been redeemed, saved, and loved by someone outside myself.* There is boundless joy in finding who we truly are and releasing and rejecting the shame and the guilt—a joy that is in no way fabricated, but genuine down to its very atoms.

We are loved beyond belief, not by someone else *out there*

210 THE ENERGY OF GOD

looking *in here* and deciding to love us despite all we may have done or not done, but because we are a part of *out there*—and not just a part of it, but a *vital* part of that whole.

We are loved because *we are that.*

We do not hate even the pinky toe of our own bodies, but we love that smallest of our parts because it is a part of our whole, and without it, our entire balance is thrown off!

Yeshua looked each person in the eye, truly listened to both what they were saying and not saying, and was fully present for them—fully human, yet fully God. Yeshua was able to look past the social statuses and outer distractions to find the heart-core of the situation, the same way we are able to look past the imagery and catchphrases of a religion or path to find the heart of its purpose, its aim and intention. His desire was to find exactly what each individual needed most, then love them by either gifting that need to them or guiding them to the truth that would bring them to the meeting of that need, whichever was most impacting and most beneficial for that unique individual. In this way, he saved them.

Yeshua as savior does not mean he literally saves us, but shows us the way to save ourselves: the way to love, and the way to end the suffering of our minds. No one can do anything else for another person; an alcoholic must be willing and ready to do the work themselves in order to break the habit of drinking. No intervention will work if they do not want it to work, or if they do not come to their own personal decision that it's time to quit drinking.

Yeshua's mission was to bring justice and balance, and to teach others how to live justly.

But Godly justice is nothing like human justice.

Human justice is making someone pay, an eye for an eye.

Godly justice is mercy and grace, an irresistibly compassionate desire to alleviate suffering and foster core-level healing.

Human justice is punitive, shunning, and branding.

Godly justice is embracing, seeing, and hearing.

Human justice is locking them away.

Godly justice is setting them free.

I can't love that way.

No matter how hard I try, I can't unconditionally love everyone no matter what they've done, I can't completely forgive every offense to myself or my family, I can't operate from a space of boundless love and acceptance in every situation.

But I'm making my Way to that place.

I'm determined to eventually arrive at that other shore.

I have to.

I cannot shake the urge, the drive, the vision.

It's who I am, at my core.

It's who *you* are, at *your* core.

Growing up, I was forced to go to church. Later, I left of my own decision; now I go back of my own decision.

But I don't go to church to get saved or feel saved or make sure I'm saved; I go to be in the atmosphere of love, to be a part of a community that is focused on this love and committed to this kingdom of love.

This is what church is.

Church is not a building or a set of rules to follow, it's a people, a community — and a community, a tribe, is extremely important in our lives. Community is a mirror of the wholeness of the Universe, the unity of the whole.

If a church/community is loving and accepting others just

as they are, inviting them in, offering them a seat at the table regardless of their present situation, on un-privileged ground out in the local community, asking about and meeting the basic, real-life needs of the neighborhood with no thought of reward or return, then that is the Kingdom. That is the Way.

If a church/community is not interested in and/or doing these things, that is not the Way—that is instead an elite member's-only club.

Evangelism and missionary work is not meant to be about converting others to a religion, changing them into being like you, it is meant to be about converting others to love, going out into the world and surrounding them, submerging them—baptizing them—with the name of love, inspiring them to awaken to what is also their own true nature: the energy of God.

Was Yeshua real? Did he really do all these things that seem like miracles to our modern minds? Did he really return to life after death? It doesn't matter—he is real now, and he is you.

My dear friends, come.

Let's love.

Come just as you are, but I can't promise you'll stay that way.

What marvelous love the Father has extended to us!
Just look at it – we're called children of God!

That's who we really are.

But that's also why the world doesn't recognize us
or take us seriously,
because it has no idea what the energy of God is
or what it's up to.

But friends,
that's exactly who we are:

the children of God.

And that's only the beginning.
Who knows how we'll end up!

What we do know is this:
when the energy of God is openly revealed,

we'll see God,

and in seeing God,
we will become like God.[15]

REVELATION

ALL THINGS NEW

MY DEAR BROTHERS AND Sisters,

May undeserved kindness be shown to you, and may you reach a peace of mind that surpasses all logic and reason. I wish these for you beyond all things, for I know you have been doing your absolute best in this world that seems to have gone mad with all manner of violence and hatefulness. You have not given up, despite your endless difficulties, and you hold your eyes to the things that remain beautiful even in the midst of these terrible times. You yourselves are in fact these things of beauty, undefeated by the world around you, insistent on shining in your beauty and your faith that this world is still a beautiful place to be, despite some outward appearances.

Hear me when I say now that you have encouraged me, even in times you thought it was only I encouraging you. All things are created with two reflections. What shines on one, shines on the other, and what is dimmed in one, dims in the other. We know this is true from the things we have seen when we were together. And I long to be together with you once again. I have every hope that this will happen, and I hold on to this hope as one of the beautiful things in this place.

My dear ones, please remember when you feel alone and in darkness that there are many others within you who also feel this darkness, just as there are those within you who feel the light and beautiful things. There is a cause for all these, and all these have their times and purposes. There are no accusations for those in darkness, just as there are no accusations for those in light. Know that whatever place you find yourself in is not an island. Know that whatever you need is always present, always within you.

There are those around us who do accuse, and who do mark others with labels and judgments for the purpose of separation. These desire the safety and comfort of existence, just as you yourselves do, but they do not understand that safety and comfort are gifts inside each of us as we understand these things. Have patience with them, and know the place they stand, not from the thinking that your own place is greater or more beautiful, but from the knowledge that you yourselves were once exactly where they are now. Remember the roads you have traveled to reach this place, and the love and encouragement you were shown as you opened your eyes. Love them the same, disregarding the words of others. We follow only the hearts that have developed within us. We know we must continue this way, for we feel the void of separation it creates within these earthly bodies when we do not.

So put love on your lips as a balm, dear brothers and sisters. Let every word from your mouth and every thought from your heart be a kiss of beauty to all creatures and all of creation. Turn nothing away, even the things that disturb your sensitive hearts, for each time you look on these things with the light of your being, you change them. And you are changing this world.

Greet everyone and everything you meet with the love and respect of an intimate family member, as you know that we have all been formed as one family.

I and all within me send you love and peace without pause.

May you find joy and encouragement in this, until we communicate again.

I love you.

It is finished.

We live in a world in which we need to share responsibility. It's easy to say, 'It's not my child, not my community, not my world, not my problem.' Then there are those who see the need and respond. I consider those people my heroes.

Fred (Mister) Rogers

Thank you,
O my Father
For giving us your Son
And leaving your Spirit
'til your work on earth is done...[16]

We have work to do.

ENDNOTES

1. Shantideva, *Bodhicaryavatara* (*The Bodhisattva's Way of Life*)
2. Psalm 139:7-12
3. I John 4:7-8, 12-13, 16-17
4. I Corinthians 13:1-3
5. *Kena Upanishad,* a Hindu sacred text, ~500 B.C.
6. Masahisa Goi, an *ukiah* (reverse haiku)
7. Galatians 5:1,13-14
8. Hafez, a 14th century Persian mystic poet
9. James 2:15-17
10. Lloyd Matthew Thompson, *The True Constant* © 2015
11. Iona, *Bird of Heaven* © 1993 Open Sky
12. Jalaluddin Rumi, a 13th century Sufi mystic poet
13. John Wesley
14. Hebrews 12:14-15, Matthew 5:9
15. I John 3:1-3
16. Keith Green, *There is a Redeemer* © 1969 Sparrow